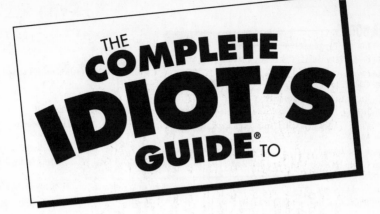

THE
COMPLETE IDIOT'S GUIDE® TO

Spanish-English Crossword Puzzles

by Gail Stein and Matt Gaffney

ALPHA

A member of Penguin Group (USA) Inc.

ALPHA BOOKS

Published by the Penguin Group

Penguin Group (USA) Inc., 375 Hudson Street, New York, New York 10014, U.S.A.

Penguin Group (Canada), 10 Alcorn Avenue, Toronto, Ontario, Canada M4V 3B2 (a division of Pearson Penguin Canada Inc.)

Penguin Books Ltd, 80 Strand, London WC2R 0RL, England

Penguin Ireland, 25 St Stephen's Green, Dublin 2, Ireland (a division of Penguin Books Ltd)

Penguin Group (Australia), 250 Camberwell Road, Camberwell, Victoria 3124, Australia (a division of Pearson Australia Group Pty Ltd)

Penguin Books India Pvt Ltd, 11 Community Centre, Panchsheel Park, New Delhi—10 017, India

Penguin Group (NZ), cnr Airborne and Rosedale Roads, Albany, Auckland 1310, New Zealand (a division of Pearson New Zealand Ltd)

Penguin Books (South Africa) (Pty) Ltd, 24 Sturdee Avenue, Rosebank, Johannesburg 2196, South Africa

Penguin Books Ltd, Registered Offices: 80 Strand, London WC2R 0RL, England

Publisher: *Marie Butler-Knight*
Editorial Director: *Mike Sanders*
Managing Editor: *Billy Fields*
Senior Acquisitions Editor: *Paul Dinas*
Production Editor: *Megan Douglass*
Copy Editor: *Michael Dietsch*
Cover Designer: *Bill Thomas*
Book Designer: *Trina Wurst*
Layout: *Ayanna Lacey*
Proofreader: *John Etchison*

Contents

Part 2:   Medium Puzzles   37

Part 3:   Difficult Puzzles   73

Appendixes

Introduction

If you're a puzzle lover and want a fun, fast way to improve your Spanish vocabulary, *The Complete Idiot's Guide to Spanish-English Crossword Puzzles* is the book for you. Set aside those flash cards and long, boring lists of vocabulary words; sharpen a pencil (with an eraser, if you think you need it); make yourself a cup of coffee or tea; and sit down with the crosswords in this book. In no time, you'll see how learning Spanish can be effortless, enjoyable, and rewarding.

The Complete Idiot's Guide to Spanish-English Crossword Puzzles is designed to help students with varying degrees of linguistic ability expand their vocabulary and attain a high level of proficiency in a language ever-increasing in popularity. The more than 100 puzzles in this book entertain and challenge while providing comprehensive, up-to-date vocabulary on topics such as food, clothing, parts of the body, synonyms, antonyms, culture, and more.

Whether you're a student, a traveler, a businessperson, or simply a lover of Spanish, this book provides you with the words you'll need to enrich your vocabulary. What are you waiting for? Turn the page and see how much fun puzzling your way to better Spanish skills can be.

¡Buena suerte! (Good luck!)

How to Use This Book

This book is divided into three parts, with the puzzles grouped by increasing levels of difficulty:

In **Part 1, "Easy Puzzles,"** most of the clues you get are in English, and you have to fill in the answers in Spanish. We give you a clue or two in Spanish in Part 1 as well, but when we do, you get an English translation along with it.

In **Part 2, "Medium Puzzles,"** the clues are still mostly in English, but they tend to be longer sentences that describe the Spanish answer word, rather than just one-word synonyms. We also work in a number of Spanish-language clues into this section—and you don't always get an English translation, so *cuidado* (be careful)!

In **Part 3, "Difficult Puzzles,"** most of the clues are in Spanish (as are all the answers, of course). You get a few clues in English in the difficult section, too, but the Spanish answers to those words are real toughies!

If you get stumped, turn to Appendix D, where you'll find all the words you need to solve every puzzle. When you've finished (or when you need a little help), you'll find the answer keys in the back of the book as well.

Acknowledgments

From Matt: I'd like to thank Christy Wagner and Megan Douglass at Alpha for reviewing the book, and Paul Dinas at Alpha for coordinating the book.

Special Thanks to the Technical Reviewer

The Complete Idiot's Guide to Spanish-English Crossword Puzzles was reviewed by an expert who double-checked the accuracy of what you'll learn here, to help us ensure that this book gives you everything you need to know about improving your Spanish the fun way—by doing crossword puzzles. Special thanks are extended to Wigberto Rivera.

Trademarks

All terms mentioned in this book that are known to be or are suspected of being trademarks or service marks have been appropriately capitalized. Alpha Books and Penguin Group (USA) Inc. cannot attest to the accuracy of this information. Use of a term in this book should not be regarded as affecting the validity of any trademark or service mark.

Easy Puzzles

Here are 34 (relatively) easy Spanish puzzles to test your vocabulary. Almost all the clues in this part's puzzles are in English, and all the answers are in Spanish. The only clues you'll run into in Spanish are parts of phrases you have to fill into the answer grid, and you'll always be given the English translation for these phrases in the clue.

Unlike a traditional book of foreign language vocabulary, you'll notice the puzzles here aren't grouped strictly by subject. For example, Puzzles #5 and #6 deal with food, but then so does, from a slightly different angle, Puzzle #14. This slight jumbling of subject matter has been adopted to more accurately reflect how a student comes upon language when learning in a foreign land—a little bit here, a little bit there, with other subjects and experiences in between. Of course, you're free to tackle the puzzles in any order you like.

¿Listo? ¡Vamos!

Puzzle #1: Asking for Directions/*Pidiendo Direcciones*

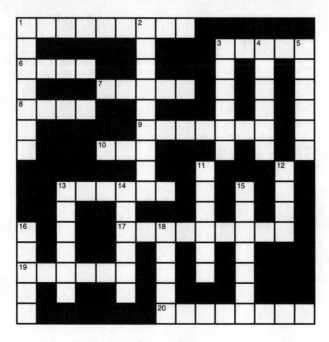

Across

1. Direction
3. To exit
6. Route
7. Intersection
8. How
9. Corner
10. South
13. City
17. Side street
19. Block
20. ___ *de* (across from)

Down

1. Right
2. Left
3. To continue
4. To arrive
5. Road sign
11. To look for
12. East
13. To cross
14. To turn
15. ___ *de* (in front of)
16. Toward
18. Street

Puzzle #2: At the Doctor's/*En el Consultorio del Doctor*

Across

1. "*Me* ___" ("I feel")
5. Flu
6. ___ *roto* (broken bone)
10. Cold
12. Rash
13. Pain
15. Asthma
16. Fever
18. *Primeros* ___ (first aid)
19. To help
20. Better

Down

2. Cough
3. Dizziness
4. Bruise
7. To sneeze
8. Worse
9. Cure
10. To recover
11. To hurt
14. Vaccination
17. Lump

Puzzle #3: At Work/*En el Trabajo*

Across

1. Insurance
5. Boss
8. Employee
9. Appointment
10. Work day
11. *Tiempo* ___ (part-time)
12. Work shift
14. Job application
15. ___ *de trabajo* (place of work)
16. Overtime pay

Down

1. Salary
2. References
3. Office
4. Worker
6. Company
7. Job
12. Degree
13. *Día* ___ (day off)

Puzzle #4: Counting/*Contando*

Across

1. One hundred
4. Four
5. Sixty
6. Third
7. Eleven
8. Zero
11. Ten
12. Sixteen
13. Five
14. Thirty
15. Three
16. One
17. Second
19. Eight
20. First
21. Six

Down

2. Nine
3. Seven
4. Fourteen
7. Eighty
9. Two hundred
10. Twenty
11. Tenth
12. Twelve
15. Thirteen
18. Two

Puzzle #5: Snacks: Fruits and Nuts/ *Bocadillos: Frutas y Nueces*

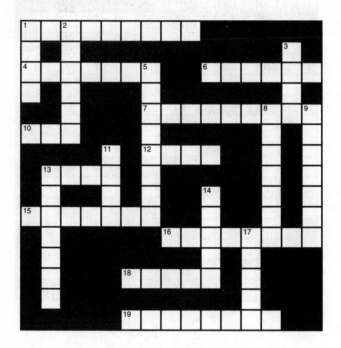

Across

1. Peanut
4. Plum
6. Watermelon
7. Peach
10. Grape
12. Walnut
13. Pear
15. Apple
16. Hazelnut
18. Fruit
19. Olive

Down

1. Coconut
2. Cherry
3. Fig
5. Almond
8. Grapefruit
9. Orange
11. Raisin
13. Plantain
14. Strawberry
17. Lemon

Puzzle #6: Meat, Fish, and Poultry/*Carne, Pescado, y Aves*

Across

3. Roast beef
6. Lamb
7. Anchovy
8. Ham
9. Seafood
11. Shrimp
13. Duck
15. Fish
18. Crab

Down

1. Lobster
2. Trout
4. Sausage
5. Pork
10. *Carne de* ___ (beef)
12. Steak
13. Chicken
14. Bacon
15. Turkey
16. Tuna
17. Oyster

Puzzle #7: In the Museum/*En el Museo*

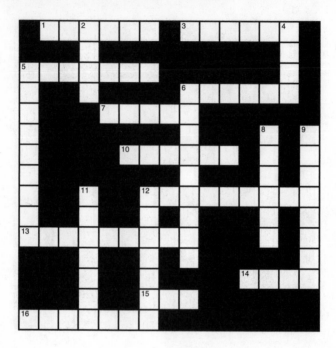

Across

1. To etch
3. Style
5. To show
6. Painting
7. Talent
10. Scene
12. Sculpture
13. Abstract
14. Work
15. Light
16. Gallery

Down

2. Art
4. *Pintura al* ___ (oil painting)
5. Muralist
6. Collection
8. Drawing
9. *Pintura de* ___ (watercolor)
11. Detail
12. School

Puzzle #8: In the Sky/*En el Cielo*

Across

1. Shadow
3. *Espacio* ___ (outer space)
9. Uranus
10. Moon
11. Rocket
14. Planet
16. Star
18. To revolve

Down

1. ___ *solar* (solar system)
2. Mercury
4. Orbit
5. Atmosphere
6. Satellite
7. Mars
8. Galaxy
11. Heaven
12. Comet
13. To shine
14. Pluto
15. Cloud
17. Sun

Puzzle #9: In the Theater/*En el Teatro*

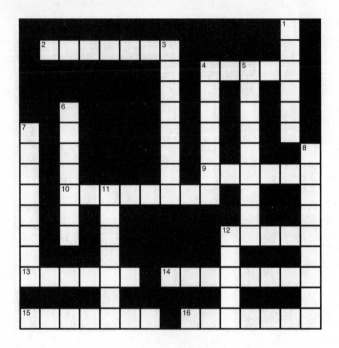

Across

2. Audience
4. Role
9. Lines
10. Set
12. Curtain
13. Actress
14. To applaud
15. Seat
16. Dialogue

Down

1. Balcony
3. Orchestra
4. Aisle
5. Character
6. Comedy
7. Tragedy
8. Stage
11. Song
12. Plot

Puzzle #10: On the Phone/*Al Teléfono*

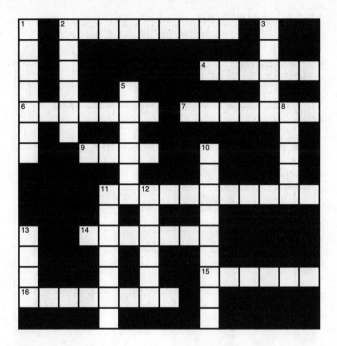

Across

2. To answer
4. *Llamada en* ___ (call waiting)
6. *Teléfono* ___ (speaker phone)
7. Busy
9. ___ *telefónica* (phone book)
11. ___ *automático* (answering machine)
14. Call
15. To hang up
16. Operator

Down

1. Message
2. ___ *del teléfono* (phone bill)
3. ___ *de servicio* (out of order)
5. ___ *de área* (area code)
8. Dial
10. *Llamada de larga* ___ (long-distance call)
11. *Teléfono* ___ (cell phone)
12. Number
13. Dial tone

Puzzle #11: Expressing Your Opinion/ *Expresando Su Opinión*

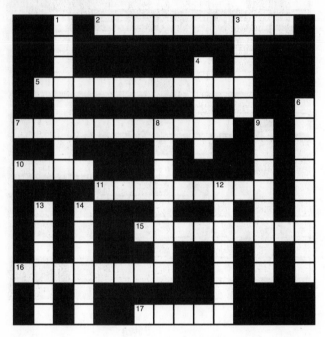

Across

2. Complicated
5. Wonderful
7. Interesting
10. Bad
11. Unbelievable
15. Amusing
16. Ridiculous
17. Great

Down

1. Childish
3. Atrocious
4. Silly
6. Disgusting
8. Boring
9. Special
12. Awesome
13. Funny
14. Super

Puzzle #12: Useful Expressions/*Expresiones Útiles*

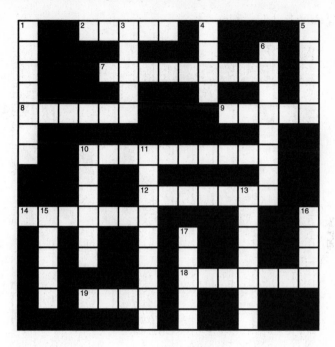

Across

2. Better
7. Amazing
8. Certain
9. Obvious
10. Enough
12. Possible
14. Absurd
18. Curious
19. Useful

Down

1. Difficult
3. Fair
4. Rare
5. Clear
6. It's advisable
10. Sure
11. Impossible
13. A pity
15. Good
16. Bad
17. Easy

Puzzle #13: In the Classroom/*En el Salón de Clase*

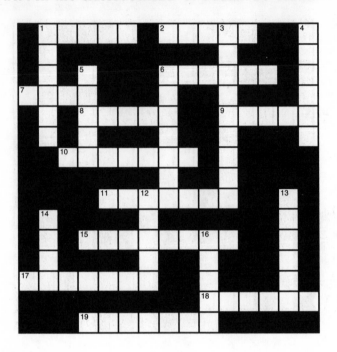

Across

1. Pen
2. Paper
6. Quiz
7. Chalk
8. Pencil
9. Class
10. Word
11. Schedule
15. Question
17. Subject
18. Test
19. Backpack

Down

1. Page
3. Exercise
4. School supplies
5. Mistake
6. Chalkboard
12. Ruler
13. Bell
14. Grade
16. Homework

Puzzle #14: In the Supermarket/*En el Supermercado*

Across

1. Bread
3. Bottle
4. Coffee
6. Yogurt
7. Nuts
10. Milk
12. Box
13. Cheese
14. Juice
15. Can
17. Bag
18. Butter

Down

1. Package
2. Candy
4. Meat
5. Fruit
8. Cream
9. Cashier
10. Vegetables
11. Eggs
15. Pound
16. Garlic

Puzzle #15: In Spanish Class/*En la Clase de Español*

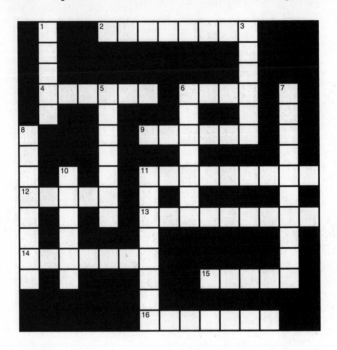

Across

2. To correct
4. To erase
6. Classroom
9. Student
11. Activity
12. Phrase
13. Answer
14. Sentence
15. *Libro de* ___ (textbook)
16. To repeat

Down

1. Verb
3. Review
5. Summary
6. *Tomar* ___ (to take notes)
7. Noun
8. Teacher
10. To speak
11. To learn

Puzzle #16: Love at First Sight/*Amor a Primera Vista*

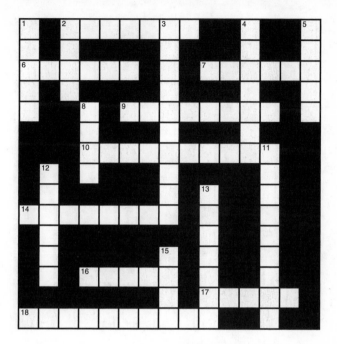

Across

2. To hug
6. Lover
7. Together
9. Funny
10. Charming
14. Friendly
16. Beloved
17. Sweet
18. Respectful

Down

1. Handsome
2. To love
3. Passionate
4. Honest
5. To kiss
8. Faithful
11. Romantic
12. Shy
13. Darling
15. Cute

Puzzle #17: Ends in *-er/Termina en* -er

Across

1. To learn
5. To understand
6. To hide
8. To read
9. To believe
10. To sweep
11. To sell
13. To promise
16. To surprise

Down

1. To agree
2. To answer
3. To break
4. To drink
5. To eat
7. To insult
12. To run
14. To insert
15. To fear

Puzzle #18: On the Menu/*En el Menú*

Across

2. Breakfast
5. Soup
8. Drinks
9. Beer
11. Snack
12. Juice
17. Omelet
18. Cheese
19. Ice cream

Down

1. Dessert
3. Lunch
4. Coffee
6. Fish
7. Eggs
10. Appetizer
13. Cracker
14. Meat
15. Pie
16. Dinner

Puzzle #19: Where?/¿Dónde?

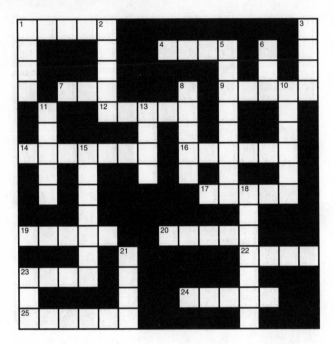

Across

1. ___ *de* (far from)
4. Before
7. For (on behalf of)
9. *En el* ___ *de* (at the bottom of)
12. Between, among
14. Right
16. Against
17. *En* ___ *de* (in the middle of)
19. Toward
20. *Al* ___ *de* (at the end of)
22. *En lo* ___ *de* (at the top of)
23. For (in order to)
24. Until
25. ___ *de* (above)

Down

1. *Al* ___ *de* (at the side of)
2. On, upon
3. Under
5. ___ *de* (opposite)
6. With
8. ___ *de* (near)
10. ___ *de* (beneath)
11. ___ *de* (outside)
13. Behind, after
15. *En la* ___ *de* (on the corner of)
18. ___ *de* (in front of)
21. *En la* ___ *de* (on the peak of)
23. *Al* ___ *de* (at the foot of)

Puzzle #20: When and How?/¿Cuándo y Cómo?

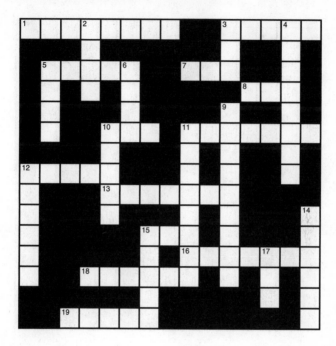

Across

1. Early
3. *Ahora* ___ (right now)
5. Now
7. Today
8. As, so
10. ___ *vez* (maybe)
11. Always
12. Better
13. Afterward
15. More
16. Still, yet
18. Soon
19. *A* ___ (sometimes)

Down

2. Worse
3. Very
4. ___ *tanto* (meanwhile)
5. Here
6. There
9. Excessively, too
10. Late
11. *Por* ___ (of course)
12. *A* ___ (often)
14. ___ *antes* (as soon as possible)
15. Less
17. *De* ___ *en cuando* (from time to time)

Puzzle #21: What Is Your Ethnicity?/¿Cuál Es Su Etnicidad?

Across

1. European
3. French
6. Venezuelan
8. African
10. White
12. Black
13. Dutch
14. English
15. Chinese

Down

1. American
2. Russian
4. Native American
5. Indian (from India)
7. Japanese
8. Arab
9. German
11. Canadian

Puzzle #22: What's the Weather?/¿Qué Tiempo Hace?

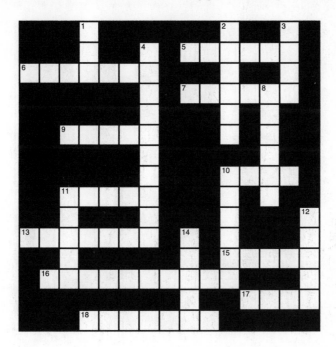

Across

5. Thunder
6. Cloudy
7. Fog
9. Snow
10. *Hace* ___ (it's cold)
11. Sky
13. Sunny
15. Climate
16. ___ *meteorológico* (forecast)
17. Dry
18. Hurricane

Down

1. *Hace* ___ (it's sunny)
2. Humid
3. Drop
4. Stormy
8. Rain
10. *Hace* ___ (it's cool)
11. *Hace* ___ (it's hot)
12. Degree
14. Breeze

Puzzle #23: Walking Outdoors/*Caminando al Aire Libre*

Across

1. Country, field
3. Desert
4. Cloud
8. Land
9. Flower
11. Lake
12. Tree
14. Forest
15. Moon
16. Plant
19. Island
20. Ocean
21. Leaf

Down

1. Hill
2. Sea
5. Star
6. Grass
7. Shore
10. Coast
12. Stream
13. Woods
16. Beach
17. Sand
18. River

Puzzle #24: Traveling/*Viajando*

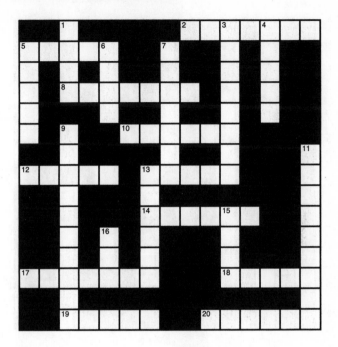

Across

2. Arrival
5. Trip
8. Bus
10. Gate
12. Boat
13. Car
14. Suitcase
17. Schedule
18. North
19. West
20. Departure

Down

1. Map
3. Luggage
4. Airplane
5. Flight
6. East
7. Cruise
9. Airport
11. Bicycle
13. Road
15. Train
16. South

Puzzle #25: Toys and Games/*Juguetes y Juegos*

Across

1. Sled
4. Wagon
7. Ball
8. *Juego de* ___ (video game)
10. Bicycle
13. ___ *de peluche* (teddy bear)
14. Checkers
15. Kite
16. Puppets

Down

1. Top
2. Playing cards
3. Jigsaw puzzle
5. To ride (a bicycle)
6. Balloon
8. Blocks
9. Magic
11. Marbles
12. Chess

Puzzle #26: When?/*¿Cuándo?*

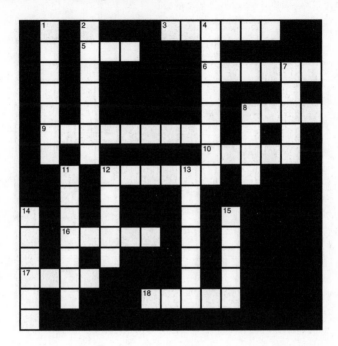

Across

3. Last
5. *A ___ de* (at about)
6. Minute
8. Hour
9. Very early morning
10. Night
12. Last
16. Before
17. *Un ___* (a while)
18. Until

Down

1. Next
2. Second
4. Early
7. Afternoon
8. Ago
11. During
12. *En ___* (exactly)
13. After
14. *Un ___ de hora* (a quarter of an hour)
15. *___ hora* (a half hour)

Puzzle #27: Quantities/*Las Cantidades*

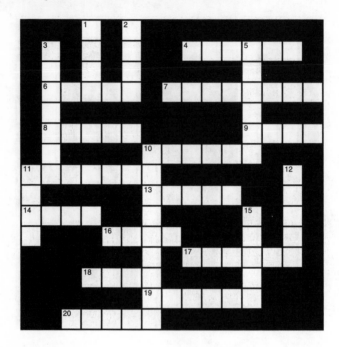

Across

4. *Un* ___ (a third)
6. *Un* ___ (a slice)
7. Enough
8. *Una* ___ (a pound)
9. *Una* ___ (a cup)
10. *Un* ___ (a tenth)
11. *Un* ___ (a package)
13. ___ *galón* (half gallon)
14. *Una* ___ (a box)
16. *Un* ___ (a glass)
17. *Un* ___ (a fifth)
18. *Una* ___ (a can)
19. *Una* ___ (a dozen)
20. *Un* ___ (a liter)

Down

1. *Un* ___ (a jar)
2. *Un* ___ (a bag)
3. *Una* ___ (a bottle)
5. *Un* ___ (a quart)
10. Too much
11. Little
12. A lot
15. *Una* ___ (a pint)

Puzzle #28: Ends in -ir/Termina en -ir

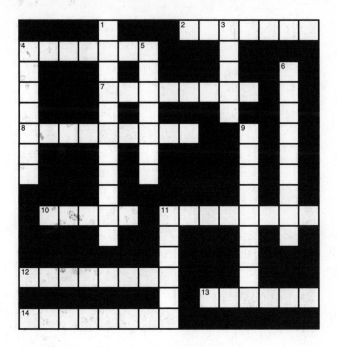

Across

2. To divide
4. To define
7. To write
8. To describe
10. To open
11. To fight
12. To permit
13. To leave
14. To prohibit

Down

1. To interrupt
3. To live
4. To decide
5. To receive
6. To discover
9. To share
11. To cover

Puzzle #29: Musical Instruments/*Instrumentos Musicales*

Across

1. Clarinet
5. Keyboard
7. Xylophone
8. Organ
11. Trombone
12. Piano
13. Piccolo
14. Drum
15. Drum set

Down

1. Horn
2. Harp
3. Cello
4. Saxophone
5. Trumpet
6. Accordion
9. Harmonica
10. Guitar
13. Flute

Puzzle #30: On the Map: Countries/*En el Mapa: Los Países*

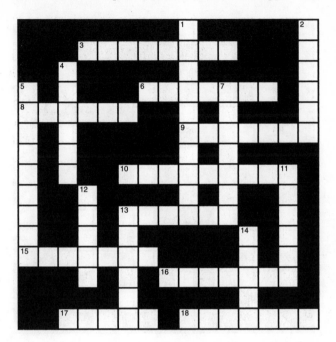

Across

3. Germany
6. Poland
8. Italy
9. Turkey
10. Morocco
13. Spain
15. Algeria
16. Belgium
17. Japan
18. ___ *Unidos* (United States)

Down

1. England
2. Greece
4. Brazil
5. Denmark
7. Norway
11. Sweden
12. Tunisia
13. Egypt
14. Switzerland

Puzzle #31: Expressing Action/*Expresando Acción*

Across

1. I see
2. She says
3. She is
4. We laugh
5. You have
7. I make
11. I bring
12. I come
13. They go
14. I give
15. I laugh
16. I am
17. I hear

Down

1. He comes
3. I am
4. He laughs
6. I go out
8. I fall
9. I put
10. We are
11. I have
13. I go
14. I say

Puzzle #32: Studying Math/*Estudiando Matemáticas*

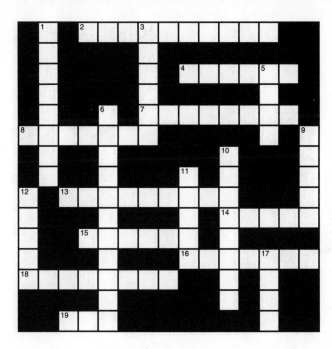

Across

2. Percent
4. To subtract
7. To solve
8. Circle
13. Triangle
14. To measure
15. Height
16. To reduce
18. Solution
19. Times

Down

1. ___ *por* (divided by)
3. Center
5. Area
6. To multiply
9. Value
10. Average
11. To add
12. Minus
17. Cone

Puzzle #33: Materials and Textures/*Materiales y Telas*

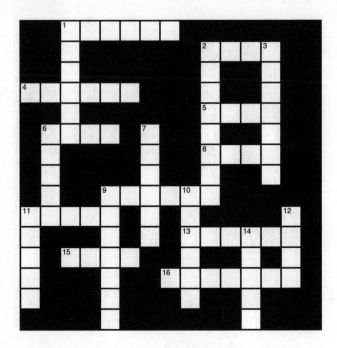

Across

1. Marble
2. Wool
4. Stone
5. Satin
6. Corduroy
8. Linen
9. Rubber
11. Copper
13. Lace
15. Fur
16. Flannel

Down

1. Wood
2. Brick
3. Cotton
6. Lead
7. Suede
9. Cement
10. Iron
11. Leather
12. Silk
14. Steel

Puzzle #34: In the Hospital/*En el Hospital*

Across

1. *Unidad de ___ intensivo* (intensive care unit)
4. Pulse
6. Accident
9. X-ray
11. ___ *de operaciones* (operating room)
12. Crutches
13. Nurse
14. *Primeros ___* (first aid)

Down

1. Surgeon
2. Cast
3. To break
4. ___ *arterial* (blood pressure)
5. Bandage
7. To cut oneself
8. Stretcher
10. To fall
12. ___ *de operaciones* (operating table)

Part **2**

Medium Puzzles

For the medium-difficulty level puzzles in this part, you'll still find most of the clues in English. But unlike the one-word clues you found in Part 1, the clues in this part are longer sentences in English that describe the Spanish word or phrase you're looking for. This helps you understand broader concepts in Spanish, as well as increase your comprehension and vocabulary—especially since we've snuck a few more Spanish-language clues in here as well.

Puzzle #35: It's Your Body/*Es Su Cuerpo*

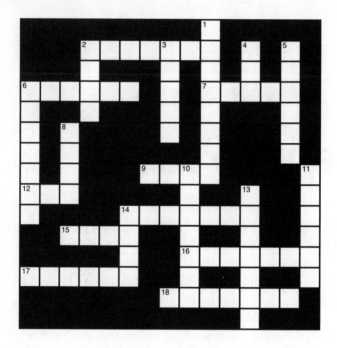

Across

2. You walk on two of these
6. Contains your brain and your face
7. You hear with this
9. You point with this
12. You see with this
14. You think with it
15. You eat and speak with this
16. Some women wear anklets around this
17. You lick stamps with this
18. Where you might carry a book bag

Down

1. Food is digested here
2. The covering of your body
3. You smell with this
4. You kick with this
5. These hang from your shoulders
6. It beats
8. You touch with this
10. They chew
11. You kiss with these
13. It bends when you run
14. Location of your eyes, ears, nose, and mouth

Puzzle #36: Let's Talk Politics/*Hablemos de Política*

Across

2. Battle between nations
6. Official elected to run a city
9. The Senate and the House of Representatives
10. The husband of a queen
12. Writes articles for the newspaper
14. Democratic or Republican, e.g.
17. Lawmaking body
18. This runs the country

Down

1. A written agreement between nations
3. Method of choosing political leaders
4. The wife of a king
5. Yea or nay
7. A rule of the government
8. The boundary between countries (border)
11. A person running for office
13. Levy imposed by the government
15. Work stoppage
16. Knowledge is ___

Puzzle #37: Looking at a Car/*Mirando un Auto*

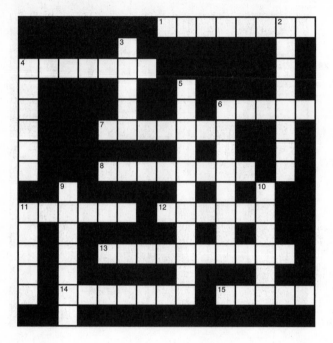

Across

1. Interior storage place (glove compartment)
4. ___ *de la puerta* (use this to open the door)
6. There are four of them
7. This furnishes an electrical current
8. Put your key here to start the car
11. You need these to stop
12. Beep this in case of emergency
13. This supplies an internal combustion engine with an explosive mixture of vaporized fuel and air

14. *Póliza de* ___ (the policy you need in case of accident)
15. ___ *de matrícula* (the plate identifying your car)

Down

2. Radiator
3. ___ *de aire* (it inflates if you have an accident)
4. Where you put gas
5. Part of the car that prevents shock or damage (bumpers)
6. What you put in your tank
9. The document that allows you to drive
10. The engine is under this (hood)
11. You turn these on at dusk

Puzzle #38: Man and Wife/*Marido y Mujer*

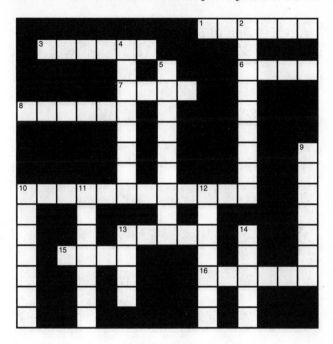

Across

1. Do the foxtrot, for example
3. ___ *de matrimonio* (wedding ring)
6. What the bride lifts to receive her first kiss
7. *Luna de* ___ (the trip the couple takes)
8. The musical instrument that plays the wedding march
10. Person who plays records for people to dance to
13. Group that plays music
15. The bride tosses this
16. Two people form this

Down

2. People asked to attend the wedding
4. The special car in which the couple rides
5. The party after the ceremony
9. Christians get married here
10. A solemn vow
11. To get married
12. You toast with this drink
13. The actual event
14. ___ *de boda* (wedding cake)

Puzzle #39: In the Bank/*En el Banco*

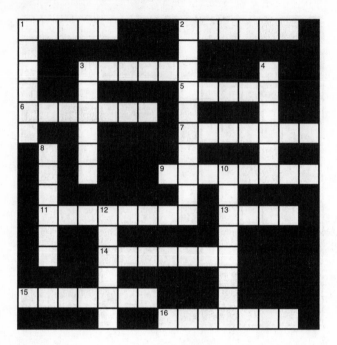

Across

1. To pay
2. The funds you have
3. To cash a check
5. The entire amount (total)
6. Extra money you receive for investing with the bank
7. The book that tells the history of your account
9. Money you borrow
11. *Dinero en* ___ (money in the form of cash)
13. ___ *fuerte* (where you keep important papers)
14. To sign the back of a check
15. What you pay at the end of the month
16. Paper money

Down

1. The cost of something
2. What you must fill out to deposit or withdraw money
3. A record of banking transactions
4. Copper or silver piece
8. Money in general
10. A division of the bank
12. Paper accepted in lieu of money

Puzzle #40: At the Beach/*En la Playa*

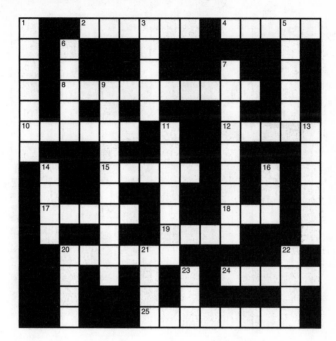

Across

2. ___ *solar* (as protection against the sun's harmful rays)
4. ___ *de sol* (protection for your eyes)
8. Too much exposure may cause this
10. ___ *de playa* (beach towel)
12. Beach sport that allows you to see flora and fauna
15. What you walk on
17. You might bring this to listen to music
18. ___ *del sol* (sunlight)
19. H_2O
20. *Flotadores para los* ___ (flotation device)
24. ___ *de playa* (ball you play with)
25. A person who rides the waves

Down

1. A sea bird
3. ___ *de surf* (a board used in the ocean)
5. Protective lotion
6. This wind comes off the sea
7. ___ *de playa* (beach umbrella)
9. Person looking out for your safety
11. Search for these on the beach
13. Atlantic or Pacific
14. This is fresh and salty at the beach
16. Sea creature
20. ___ *de sol* (what to do when you're not swimming)
21. The movement of water
22. ___ *de playa* (beach clothing)
23. Mediterranean or Caribbean

Puzzle #41: At the Hairdresser's/*En la Peluquería*

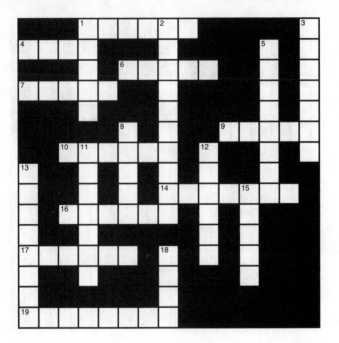

Across

1. This is used to clean your hair
4. It grows on your head
6. This grows on a man's chin
7. What you ask for to color your hair
9. To blow hair with a dryer
10. ___ *facial* (facial)
14. It's used to cut your hair
16. This grows above a man's upper lip and below his nose
17. Curly
19. Describing hair that is neither straight nor curly

Down

1. The cut
2. A style where your hair is chemically curled
3. This man cuts men's hair
5. Getting your fingernails done
8. A chestnut brown hair color
11. The action of taking hair off a man's face
12. A reddish hair color
13. *En* ___ (a blunt haircut)
15. The color of yellowish hair
18. Used to set your hair

Puzzle #42: Me, Myself, and I/Yo, Yo Mismo, y Yo

Across

4. *Yo me* ___ (I take a shower)
7. *Yo me* ___ (I remember)
9. *Yo me* ___ (I feel)
10. *Yo me* ___ (I forget)
12. *Yo me* ___ (I make up my mind)
14. *Yo me* ___ (I become bored)
16. *Yo me* ___ (I am glad)
18. *Yo me* ___ (I wash myself)
20. *Yo me* ___ (I put on)

Down

1. *Yo me* ___ (I dry myself)
2. *Yo me* ___ (My name is)
3. *Yo me* ___ (I remain)
5. *Yo me* ___ (I become tired)
6. *Yo me* ___ (I hide)
8. *Yo me* ___ (I have fun)
11. *Yo me* ___ (I get up)
13. *Yo me* ___ (I fall asleep)
15. *Yo me* ___ (I break, as a part of the body)
17. *Yo me* ___ (I laugh)
19. *Yo me* ___ (I go away)

Puzzle #43: Playing Sports/*Jugando a los Deportes*

Across

1. Get the puck in the goal
5. Take the chairlift
6. On rollers or ice
7. A sport played with a bat and a ball
13. Love–15
15. You go underwater to see the flora and fauna
16. Running around in circles
18. Get the ball in the goal, but don't touch it with your hands

Down

2. Riding horseback
3. You wear gloves and try to knock out your opponent
4. You need a bike to do this
8. A sport in which you shoot hoops
9. Get a strike or a spare!
10. Hit the ball over the net with your hands
11. Off to the pool
12. Looking for tuna
14. A bogey, a birdie, an eagle, or just plain par
17. Using oars

Puzzle #44: Preparing a Meal/*Preparando una Comida*

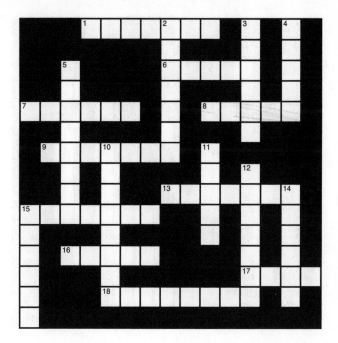

Across

1. To sauté meat
6. To chop meat or vegetables
7. To cut meat or vegetables
8. To fry meat or vegetables
9. To mix ingredients
13. To cook a meal
15. To bake in the oven
16. To beat ingredients together
17. To roast meat or vegetables
18. To stir ingredients in a pot

Down

2. To bread a cutlet
3. To pour a liquid
4. To cover what you're cooking
5. To melt an ingredient such as chocolate
10. To heat a meal
11. To boil vegetables, meat, or an egg
12. To chill an ingredient
14. To grate an ingredient such as cheese
15. To boil a liquid

Puzzle #45: Members of the Family/*Miembros de la Familia*

Across

5. Your male offspring
6. A male offspring
7. Your sister's daughter
9. Your uncle's wife
11. Your female sibling
12. The woman you married
15. Your father's father
16. Your wife's mother
17. Your child's male child

Down

1. Your daughter's husband
2. The son of your mother's sister
3. Your aunt's husband
4. Your female parent
5. Your male sibling
6. Your child's female child
8. Your son's female friend
10. Your mother's mother
12. The man you married
13. Your male parent
14. Your husband's father

Puzzle #46: Traveling by Plane/*Viajando por Avión*

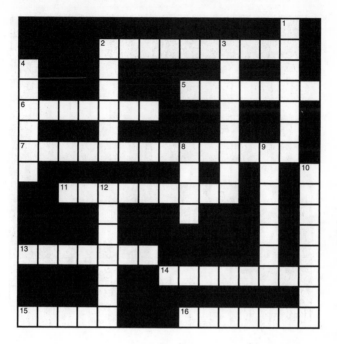

Across

2. Kennedy or LaGuardia
5. Where you're sitting
6. When you are expected to arrive
7. You put your carry-on luggage overhead in one of these
11. Aeroméxico, for example
13. Where you walk on a plane between the rows of seats
14. Your suitcases
15. A scheduled trip by plane
16. Where you're going

Down

1. A person at the airport who helps you with your baggage
2. Where you have to declare what you've purchased
3. You put this on your luggage to identify it as yours
4. If you have to change planes, you don't want to miss this
8. *Equipaje de* ___ (your suitcases)
9. ___ *de embarque* (the pass you need to get on your flight)
10. A traveler on a plane
12. ___ *de equipaje* (where you get your suitcases)

Puzzle #47: In the Clothing Store/*En la Tienda de Ropa*

Across

1. *Me* ___ (it fits me)
4. The cost
6. The size of clothing
8. *Es* ___ (it's narrow)
11. A reduction in price
12. Size for the biggest person
13. *Es* ___ (it's long)
16. Opposite of expensive
17. ___ *de crédito* (card that allows you to pay without spending cash)
18. Size for the average person

Down

2. *Es* ___ (it's tight)
3. Élan, flair, panache
5. A large retail store organized into departments
7. The person who helps you
9. *Es* ___ (it's baggy)
10. The shop window
14. *Me* ___ (I like it)
15. The opposite of inexpensive

Puzzle #48: On the Computer/*En el Ordenador*

Across

2. You want a high-speed one to log on to the Internet quickly
4. Use this to move the cursor
6. To transfer data (download)
8. ___ *inicial* (homepage)
10. The screen or monitor
11. You use this to save your place (bookmark)
12. ___ *central* (central processing unit)
15. It contains all the keys (keyboard)
16. A unit of memory (byte)

Down

1. ___ electrónico (e-mail)
2. The virtual world of the Internet
3. A computer glitch (bug)
5. The person using the computer
7. Someone who hacks into a computer
9. The ink reservoir for your printer (cartridge)
13. *Base de* ___ (database)
14. A pictorial representation

Puzzle #49: Eating Vegetables/*Comiendo Legumbres*

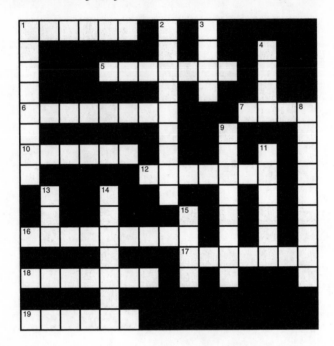

Across

1. The "hot house" variety of this green vegetable has no seeds
5. Endive
6. Popeye claimed this made him strong
7. This yellow vegetable is sometimes served on the cob
10. Tomato
12. This white vegetable is a bulb
16. Hearts of these are often used in a salad
17. This green vegetable has florets
18. Vegetable
19. These beans are green

Down

1. This salad vegetable comes in colors: red, yellow, orange, and green
2. Little green vegetables are served with carrots
3. This green vegetable grows in stalks (celery)
4. This vegetable is also called a spud (potato)
8. Eat this orange vegetable and you'll have good night vision
9. This white vegetable often describes a boxer's ear
11. This dark red salad vegetable has a white interior and is eaten raw
13. Corned beef is often served with this
14. This green, leafy vegetable serves as the bed for salad
15. Turnip

Puzzle #50: At the Stationery Store/*En la Papelería*

Across

4. Used to tie packages
5. Case used to hold pens and pencils
9. ___ *de papel* (pad used for writing)
10. Graphite writing implement
12. Use this to sharpen a pencil
14. Used to staple together sheets of paper
16. A fountain pen
17. Shows you the months and the dates

Down

1. Stick these in a peg board
2. Fluid in a pen
3. *Notas* ___ (sticky notes used as flags)
6. Item used to cut
7. *Papel de* ___ (paper used to wrap packages)
8. Clip used to hold paper together
11. Put a letter in this to mail it
13. You write on a sheet of this
14. Used to erase mistakes
15. ___ *de papeles* (where you throw away unwanted paper)

Puzzle #51: At Home/A Casa

Across

1. Where formal meals are served
5. Where you hang your clothes
6. What you look out of
7. Where you light a fire
9. The place that contains all the rooms
10. You walk on it
11. Where you sit in the summer to have a barbecue
12. Part of the downstairs of a house where people store things
14. You close it when you want privacy
15. Part of the upstairs of a house where people store things
16. An informal room where people often entertain their friends and watch TV

Down

1. A house or apartment is divided into these
2. Where you sleep
3. A formal living area
4. Where you park your car
8. 3C or 1A
9. Where meals are cooked
11. One of four in a room
13. Where you find the sink, toilet, and bathtub

Puzzle #52: In the Stores/*En las Tiendas*

Across

1. Where you'd go to rent a movie
4. We're having meat for dinner, so here's where I'm going
6. Buy almost any kind of food here
10. Buy a diamond ring here
11. Flowers can be purchased here
12. Want fruit? Go here
13. Get new glasses here

Down

2. When you need milk, go here
3. Treat your child to a toy here
5. Here's where I buy sweet things
7. Hungry for bread? Go here
8. *Tienda de equipo* ___ (get sports equipment here)
9. For the latest best-seller, go here

Puzzle #53: Opposite Things/*Cosas Opuestas*

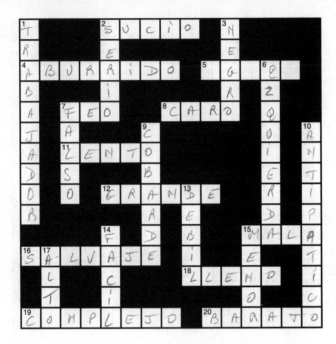

Across

2. Limpio
4. Interesante
5. Dulce
7. Hermoso
8. Barato
11. Rápido
12. Pequeño
15. Buena
16. Doméstico
18. Vacío
19. Simple
20. Caro

Down

1. Perezoso
2. Cómico
3. Blanco
6. Derecha
7. Auténtico
9. Valiente
10. Simpático
13. Fuerte
14. Difécil
15. Mayor
17. Bajo

Puzzle #54: In the Hotel/*En el Hotel*

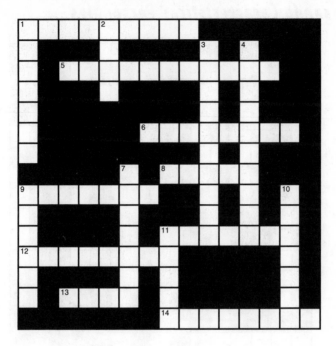

Across

1. Where you check in and out
5. It wakes you up
6. A small hotel
8. You may wash yourself here instead of in the bathtub
9. The person who carries your bags to your room
11. What you may receive if you're not in your room to answer the phone
12. *Piscina* ___ (when it's raining or cold out, swim here)
13. Where you sleep
14. A fluffy cushion used to support the head of a sleeping person

Down

1. *Tienda de* ___ (where you purchase gifts)
2. The floor on which your room is located
3. Your accommodation
4. The maid service
7. What you need to reserve a room
9. You get a view of the outdoors when you stand here
10. A person staying at the hotel
11. It's on the bed to keep you warm

Puzzle #55: Expressing Personal Characteristics/ *Expresando Características Personales*

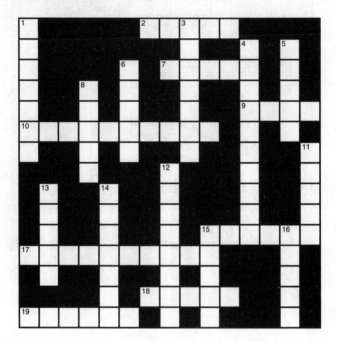

Across

2. Not young
7. Having blond hair
9. It covers your body
10. Being messy
15. Showing cynicism
17. The way you look
18. Little dots on your face or body
19. Being stout

Down

1. Being thin
3. *Bien* ___ (well mannered)
4. Your physique or build
5. Not old
6. Showing happiness
8. Having straight hair
11. Beyond pretty
12. Your moral fiber
13. Having good looks
14. The way you act toward things
15. Gray hair
16. Bald

Puzzle #56: Hobbies/*Pasatiempos*

Across

1. A musical performance
7. You see films there
8. Game with checkmate
9. ___ *de toros* (where you'll see a matador)
11. Place for art exhibits
14. Deck for many games
17. A trek in the mountains
18. *Parque de* ___ (you can ride a Ferris wheel there)

Down

2. ___ *comercial* (a large group of stores in one place)
3. Where you see a play
4. *Día de* ___ (holiday)
5. You can see different kinds of fish there
6. Where you surf
9. A puzzle like this
10. You say "king me" in this game
12. Part of a play
13. The big top
15. Going for a stroll
16. The cha-cha or the tango

Puzzle #57: Expressing Your Feelings/ *Expresando Sus Sentimientos*

Across

1. Held dear
3. Feeling very frightened
7. Uneasy and out of sorts
8. Not happy
12. Distressed about something
13. Having confidence
14. Doubting someone or something
15. Feeling calm

Down

1. Feeling upbeat
2. Not caring
3. Extremely tired
4. Eagerly desirous of something
5. Not interested
6. Showing interest or curiosity
9. Feeling thwarted despite one's best efforts
10. Desirous of what someone else has
11. Feeling very angry

Puzzle #58: How Do You Like Your Meal?/ *¿Te Gusta la Comida?*

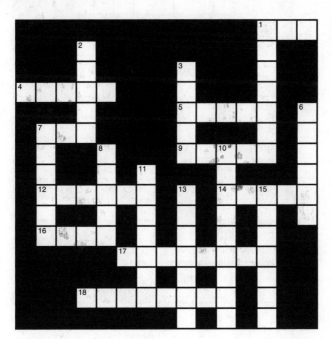

Across

1. *Sin* ___ (without salt)
4. *Lo prefiero casi* ___ (I prefer it very rare)
5. Baked in the oven
7. *Con* ___ (with garlic)
9. *No muy* ___ (not too sour)
12. Boiled in water
14. *Lo prefiero al* ___ (I prefer it steamed)
16. *Lo prefiero un poco* ___ (I prefer it medium rare)
17. *A la* ___ (broiled on the barbecue)
18. *Ligeramente* ___ (lightly breaded)

Down

1. *Lo prefiero* ___ (I prefer it tasty)
2. *Lo prefiero término* ___ (I prefer it medium)
3. *Sin* ___ (without fat)
6. *Con* ___ (with rosemary)
7. *Sin* ___ (without sugar)
8. ___ *en aceite* (fried in oil)
10. *Me gustan los huevos* ___ (I like scrambled eggs)
11. *Con* ___ (with mustard)
13. *Con* ___ (with herbs)
15. *No muy* ___ (not too spicy)

Puzzle #59: I Get Emotional/*Me Pongo Sentimental*

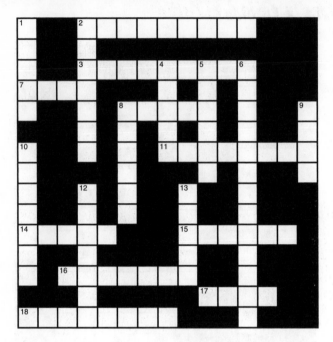

Across

2. Emotion when you're hopeful
3. Emotion when you're happy
7. Emotion when you hate
8. Emotion when you're jealous
11. Emotion when you really dislike something
14. Emotion when you're desirous of something
15. Emotion when you're angry
16. Emotion when you're feeling pride
17. Emotion when you're in love
18. Emotion when you're dejected

Down

1. Emotion when you're grieving
2. Emotion when you're elated
4. Emotion when you're guilty
5. Emotion when you feel contempt
6. Emotion when you feel despair
8. Emotion when you're brave
9. Emotion when you feel pity
10. Emotion when you're envious
12. Emotion when you're joyful
13. Emotion when you're fearful

Puzzle #60: In the Movies and on Television/ *En el Cine y en la Televisión*

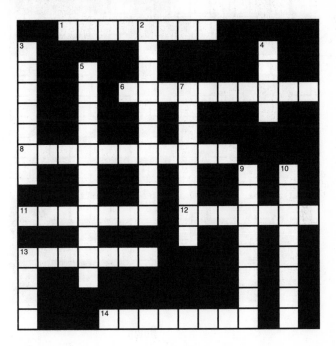

Across

1. A whodunit movie
6. What you watch to know the weather
8. Word for a broadcast
11. It's funny
12. An ad
13. Tells when the movie starts
14. Indiana Jones–style movie

Down

2. When a host speaks with a guest
3. What you buy to get into the movies
4. *Palomitas de ___* (what people eat at the movies)
5. These stories continue every day
7. This show tells what happened today
9. In the movie theater, you watch a big one of these
10. *Dibujos ___* (animated movies)
13. You need to know this if you don't want to miss the beginning of a movie

Puzzle #61: Wearing Clothing/*Llevando Ropa*

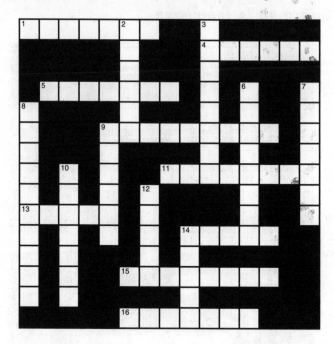

Across

1. Part of a three-piece suit
4. One of these over your clothes keeps you warm in winter
5. A woman wears one of these when she dresses formally
9. These open-toed shoes are worn in the summer
11. You wear it around your waist to hold up your pants
13. A businessman wears one to work every day
14. When it's cold out, you want these on your feet
15. Informal pants that are comfortable and blue
16. You wear these on your feet

Down

2. A man wears one of these tucked into his suit pants
3. Worn by men and women to keep their legs warm
6. A short coat to keep you warm
7. This goes around your neck to keep you warm
8. You wear these on your feet inside your shoes
9. This may be a pullover or a button-down
10. Put these on your hands to keep them warm
12. A woman wears this with a blouse
14. A woman wears this with a skirt

Puzzle #62: Using Beauty Products/ Usando Productos de Belleza

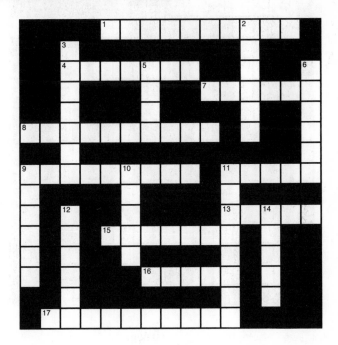

Across

1. Pins used to hold hair in place
4. Polish that covers the nails
7. ___ de labios (shiny gloss that covers the lips)
8. ___ de ojos (liner that empha- sizes the eyes)
9. ___ labial (protection for the lips)
11. Makeup applied to the face to moisturize it
13. ___ de labios (lip coloring)
15. Where you may put eyeliner
16. Coloring that's put on hair
17. Lipstick, blush, eyeliner, etc.

Down

2. Creamy cosmetic applied to the skin
3. You style your hair with this
5. Files the nails
6. Gooey product that aids in styling the hair
9. Pulverized substance used on the cheeks to give them color
10. They may get colored with a pencil
11. Makeup applied to the cheeks for color
12. ___ de ojos (shadow that's applied to the eyes)
14. You comb your hair with this

Puzzle #63: Choosing Colors/*Escogiendo Colores*

Across

2. The color of freshly fallen snow
4. The opposite of dark
5. The color of an elephant
6. A dark red
9. *Azul* ___ (the Navy's idea of blue)
10. Don't let a ___ cat cross your path!
11. The color of a matador's cape
12. A pale or light color
13. The color of an orange
15. The opposite of light
16. One of the colors in the rainbow

Down

1. The color of your tongue
2. The opposite of dull
3. A royal color
7. The color of grass
8. The color of the sun
12. The color of dirt
14. The color of the sky on a clear day

Puzzle #64: Earning a Living/*Ganándose la Vida*

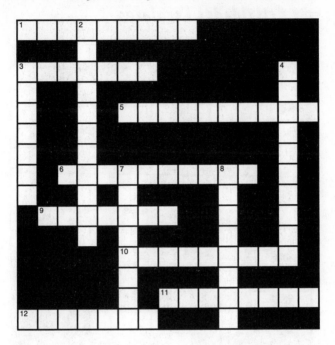

Across

1. A person who helps you with your problems
3. A person who fixes leaks
5. Someone who writes for a newspaper
6. Someone who saves lives at the pool
9. Person who carries your bags in a hotel
10. A person representing a foreign country
11. A person who does IRS returns
12. A person who sells books

Down

2. A person who owns a business
3. *Empleado* ___ (a civil service worker)
4. A person who coaches
7. A salesperson
8. Person who assists an executive

Puzzle #65: School Subjects and Activities/ *Materias y Actividades Escolares*

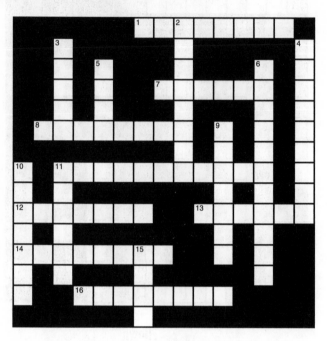

Across

1. The study of life
7. Tra la la …
8. You learn to make money
11. Where you learn word processing
12. You have to know proofs
13. Field for Newton and Einstein
14. Biology, chemistry, physics, etc.
16. The facts of the past

Down

2. Do you play the violin?
3. A group of students
4. Where in the world?
5. Everybody sing!
6. Doing calculations
9. Working with the elements
10. It'll help you in Paris
11. London's language
15. Can you paint?

Puzzle #66: Playing Baseball/*Jugando al Béisbol*

Across

1. The person who throws the ball to the catcher
2. The catcher uses this
5. Player in the outfield
6. The person who referees the game
8. One of four on the field
9. What the batter tries to hit
11. Someone who plays baseball
12. Another name for a game
13. What the player must do after he hits the ball
14. The base behind the pitcher

Down

1. First base to run to
2. ___ *de béisbol* (part of the uniform worn on the head)
3. Botched ground ball, for example
4. The player who catches the ball from the pitcher
5. Successful at-bat
7. Player hitting the ball
8. What the batter uses
10. The last base before home
11. When the batter hits one out of the park
12. Home plate

Puzzle #67: Using Furniture and Appliances/ Usando Muebles y Aparatos

Across

2. You cook on top of it
5. It indicates the time
7. Where you put folded clothes
9. A large piece of furniture in the living room
10. It covers the floor from wall to wall
11. You bake in it
12. Where you put your clothes to dry
13. It keeps foods frozen
14. It's used to make a smoothie

Down

1. You wash your clothes in it
2. A special sound system that plays music
3. You watch programs on it
4. Where you sleep
5. It keeps your food cold
6. It washes the dishes
8. It sucks up dust
12. A place to sit

Puzzle #68: Baby Talk/*Habla de Bebés*

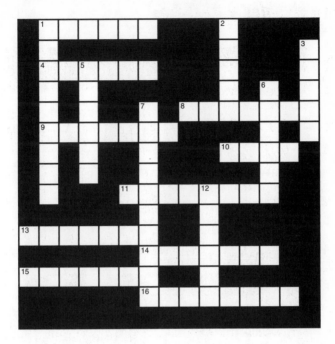

Across

1. ___ *para bebés* (special food for a baby)
4. What covers a baby in its carriage
8. ___ *de seguridad para bebés* (what a baby sits in in a car)
9. *Libro de* ___ (what's read to a child)
10. Where a baby sleeps
11. What a baby sleeps in
13. A baby sucks on this when it's tired or unhappy
14. What a baby drinks from
15. *Animal de* ___ (a toy a baby plays with)
16. You shake this to make a baby smile

Down

1. What a baby is put in for a walk
2. This moves slowly over a baby's crib
3. It keeps a baby dry
5. What is put around a baby's neck while it's eating
6. ___ *de leche* (baby's tooth)
7. What a baby is carried in
12. Person who watches a baby

Part 3

Difficult Puzzles

Ready for the toughest puzzles in the book? These will really give your Spanish a test, so don't be reluctant to use the "Word Finders" appendix in the back of the book to help you make your way.

Most of the clues in the puzzles in this part are in Spanish. This gives you an extra challenge and forces you to think conceptually and abstractly in another language. A few of the puzzles have clues in English, but these are generally puzzles that have complex vocabulary, so even with having the clues in English, you'll still feel challenged.

Buena suerte!

Puzzle #69: In the Garden/*En el Jardín*

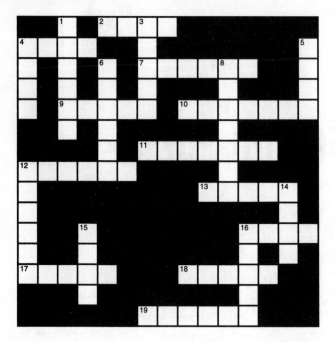

Across

2. The wood from this tree is used in furniture and flooring
4. Part of a tree that's beneath the ground
7. A small lake
9. Water-soaked soil
10. White, pink, or purple greenhouse plant
11. A purple flower
12. A stone
13. The slender part of a flower that supports it
16. Leaves are at the end of this
17. Oak or elm
18. A tulip comes from this
19. Water shoots out of this

Down

1. Green animal food that covers the ground
3. A plant that lives in the desert
4. A beautiful flower with thorns
5. This tree bears cones and nuts
6. What you must do to your lawn before it gets too overgrown
8. The outer covering of a tree
12. A flower, bush, or tree
14. Shade tree that can get a "Dutch" disease
15. Rose or tulip
16. This great tree grows from a little acorn

Puzzle #70: Getting Services/*Consiguiendo Servicios*

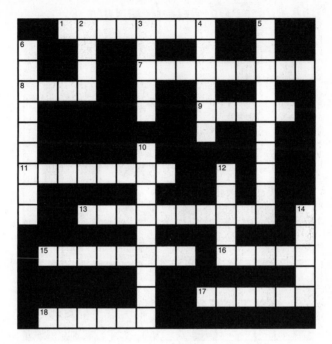

Across

1. What you have to do to a problem when you have one
7. A watch cannot do this if its battery is dead
8. *Lavar en* ___ (when the label says dry clean only, you must do this)
9. You don't want to have one missing on your shirt
11. A tailor is paid to do this to torn clothing
13. Where you wash your clothes
15. What you have when something isn't right
16. Jewelry that tells time
17. Opposite of "to buy"
18. Result of a spill

Down

2. What a cigarette burn will leave
3. What you wear over your eyes to see
4. This shows that you've paid
5. Where clothes get dry cleaned
6. This results when you catch your clothes on a nail
10. The place where you go to get your shoes repaired
12. What stores do in the morning
14. When you get a tear in a fine suit, the tailor does this

Puzzle #71: Buying a Residence/ Comprando una Residencia Domicilio

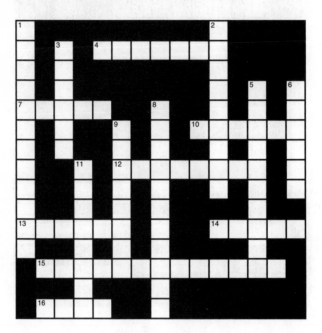

Across

4. What you need to have to obtain a mortgage
7. ___ *prestado* (the opposite of "to lend")
10. ___ *raíces* (property consisting of houses and land)
12. If you don't have enough cash, you have to take out one of these
13. The person who shows you a piece of real estate
14. Where you save money
15. What keeps a house cold in the summer
16. A dwelling that serves as living quarters for one or more families

Down

1. Power that runs machines and appliances
2. When you need a mortgage, the first thing to do is this
3. When your signature is needed, you must do this
5. Housing where each unit is individually owned
6. First, you have to do this before you find a new house
8. When the weather is cold, this keeps the house warm
9. What you pay monthly when you own a home
11. ___ *clasificados* (advertisements for property can be found here in the newspaper)

Puzzle #72: Driving a Car/*Conduciendo un Auto*

Across

2. Sometimes it forms an "S"
4. *Tener ___ de paso* (to have the right of way)
7. Use this to start the car
10. What happens when two cars collide
12. The edge of the sidewalk
13. The person at the wheel
16. What you do at the end of a trip
17. *Goma de ___* (you need this in case of a flat)
18. You need this to change a flat

Down

1. *___ de conducir* (the paperwork you must have to be able to drive)
2. A hill in the road
3. How fast you're going
5. This is where pedestrians should cross
6. A hole in the road
8. You should do this when entering a highway
9. Acura, Cadillac, or Porsche
11. Green light, yellow light, red light
14. *De sentido ___* (you can only go in one direction)
15. What you receive if you don't obey the rules of the road

Puzzle #73: Identifying Spanish-Speaking Cities/ *Identificando las Ciudades Hispanohablantes*

Across

3. La capital del Perú, fundada por Pizarro
5. La capital de Nicaragua
6. La capital de Uruguay
10. Destino turístico más conocido de México
11. ___ San Lucas (ciudad turística mexicana, situada en el extremo de la Península de Baja California)
14. La capital de Chile
15. La ___ (la capital de Cuba)
16. La ciudad española donde se encuentra la tumba de Cristóbal Colón

Down

1. La capital de Ecuador, situada al pie de un volcán
2. La capital de Colombia
4. Un puerto en el Pacífico, famoso por sus playas
5. La capital de España
7. La ciudad española conocida por sus naranjas
8. El puerto principal de España
9. La capital de Puerto Rico
10. La capital política y comercial de Venezuela
12. La ciudad española que es el centro de la industria minera del norte
13. La capital de Bolivia

Puzzle #74: In the Dictionary/*En el Diccionario*

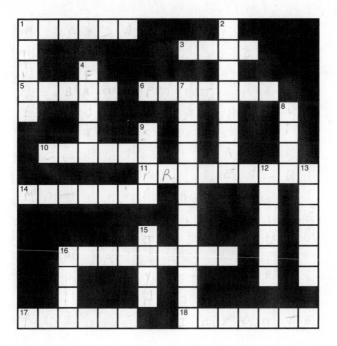

Across

1. El té es una ___
3. Una almendra es una ___
5. Un diccionario es un ___
6. "La Joconda" es una ___
10. La cocina es un ___
11. Contable es una ___
14. La geografía es una ___
16. "El Diario" es un ___
17. El flan es un ___
18. El baloncesto es un ___

Down

1. La rumba es un ___
2. La zanahoria es una ___
4. La frambuesa es una ___
7. Cubano es una ___
8. El tinto es un ___
9. El gazpacho es una ___
12. El italiano es un ___
13. Francisco es un ___ masculino
15. Un diamante es una ___
16. Los Estados Unidos son un ___

Puzzle #75: It's the Same Action/*Es la Misma Acción*

Across

4. Conducir
5. Limpiar
6. Conversar
8. Detestar
9. Ascender
11. Observar
14. Utilizar
15. Demandar
16. Elevar
17. Contemplar
18. Acabar

Down

1. Silenciar
2. Laborar
3. Partir
7. Responder
8. Conseguir
9. Continuar
10. Descender
12. Encontrar
13. Tomar

Puzzle #76: It's the Same Thing/*Es la Misma Cosa*

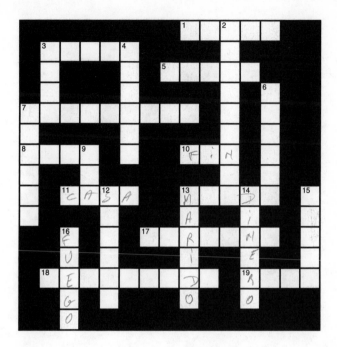

Across
1. Impuesto
3. Combate
5. Notificación
7. Hábito
8. Camarero
10. Conclusión
11. Habitación
13. Temor
17. Individuo
18. Consecuencia
19. Ceremonia

Down
2. Habitante
3. Opulencia
4. Estudiante
6. Costo
7. Alteración
9. Onda
12. Idioma
13. Esposo
14. Moneda
15. Placer
16. Incendio

Puzzle #77: Learning Culture/*Aprendiendo la Cultura*

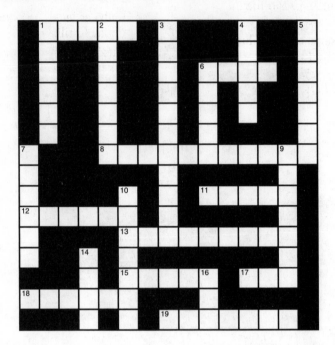

Across

1. Federico García Lorca escribió un ___ , "La casa de Bernarda Alba"
6. La unidad monetaria de México es el ___
8. Salvador Dalí perteneció a la escuela ___
11. Cantinflas fue un ___ mexicano
12. Don Quijote es una ___ escrita por Miguel de Cervantes
13. En Brasil no hablan español, hablan ___
15. Antes de cenar, los españoles comen aperitivos llamados ___
17. El Guadalquivir es el ___ más navegable de España
18. El plato de arroz, pollo, mariscos, salchichas y varios condimentos se conoce como ___
19. Diego Rivera se dedicó a pintar ___ que adornan muchos edificios públicos en México

Down

1. Una piñata contiene ___
2. Las ___ son hechas de calabazas secas con granos de maíz adentro
3. Cristóbal Colón fue conocido como el ___ de América
4. El Prado es un ___ en Madrid
5. La fruta mas famosa de Valencia es la ___

Down (continued)

6. Rubén Darío fue un ___ nicaragüense
7. Ponce de León buscó la ___ de la Juventud
9. La industria principal de las Islas Baleares es el ___

10. San Juan es la ___ de Puerto Rico
14. Cuba es la ___ más grande de las Antillas
16. México esta situado al ___ de los Estados Unidos

Puzzle #78: Listen to the Teacher/*Escuchen al Profesor*

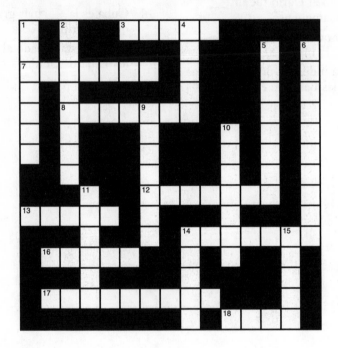

Across

3. No ___ a la puerta
7. ___ la respuesta correcta
8. Hay una prueba; ___ los libros
12. ___ sus libros cada diá
13. ___ la pizarra
14. Siempre ___ atención
16. ___ las instrucciones
17. ___ las preguntas
18. ___ responsables

Down

1. ___ a la página 15
2. ___ a la profesora
4. ___ la puerta
5. No terminen!
6. ___ las palabras del vocabulario
9. ___ las palabras después de mí
10. ___ a tiempo cada día
11. ___ aqui—cuando quieran hablarme
14. ___ permiso sólamente cuando sea necesario
15. Hay un examen, pero es fácil; no ___ nerviosos

Puzzle #79: Send It by Mail/*Envíelo por Correo*

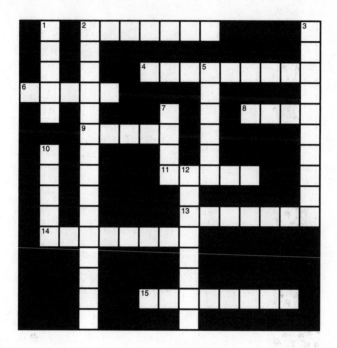

Across

2. A postal worker
4. The location of where you're sending a letter
6. Where you insert your letter
8. ___ *postal* (your zip code)
9. Your letter must have one of these on it if you want it to be delivered
11. *Correo* ___ (the fastest way to send mail overseas)
13. ___ *postal* (a card sent when you're on vacation)
14. If your letter or package is valuable, you must do this to it
15. The cost of sending a letter

Down

1. The box where you drop your letters for mailing
2. Letter writing is referred to as this
3. The window where you purchase your stamps
5. You put a letter in a mailbox to do this to it
7. ___ *de sellos* (a sheet of stamps)
10. It might start "Dear John"
12. It's up to the mailman to do this with your letters and packages

Puzzle #80: Animals/*Animales*

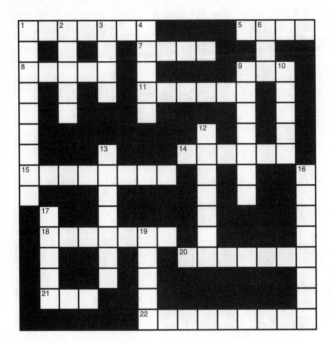

Across

1. Animal utilizado como montura o animal de tiro
5. Mamífero carnívoro de la familia de los felinos. Es muy útil en las casas como cazador de ratones
7. Animal que nos da la leche
8. Animal pequeño que nos da carne
9. Animal vertebrado acuático
11. Animal con un cuello muy largo y una cabeza pequeña
14. Animal con orejas muy grandes; el símbolo de la Pascua

15. Felino grande con manchas negras, redondas, y regularmente distribuidas en todo el en cuerpo
18. Animal roedor (*rodent*), de pelaje rojizo y cola larga y ancha. Se cría en los bosques
20. Mamífero marino que habita principalmente en los mares polares
21. Carnívoro con pelaje pardo y cabeza grande
22. Reptil sin extremidades

Down

1. Reptil grande cubierto de escamas (*scales*) que vive en las regiones intertropicales

Down (continued)

2. Un asno

3. El rey de la jungla

4. Animal que nos da la lana

6. Vertebrado volador cubierto de plumas

9. Especie de leopardo negro

10. Animal carnívoro que caza con gran astucia toda clase de animales pequeños

12. Reptil de cuerpo corto cubierto de una caparazón (*shell*)

13. Hembra (*female*) del gallo, de menor tamaño

16. Animal de color gris, con una trompa

17. Ave doméstica de cresta roja, que despierta a la gente cuando cacarea (*crows*)

19. Animales salvajes parecidos al perro, de orejas erguidas (*erect*) y cola larga

Puzzle #81: In the City/*En la Ciudad*

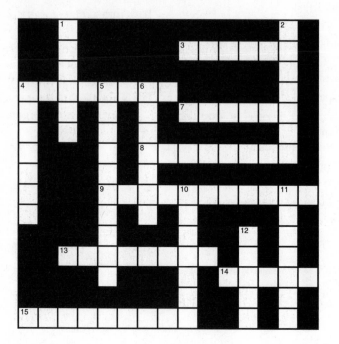

Across

3. Un lugar con una variedad de árboles y plantas, destinado al recreo
4. Se vende medicina en una
7. Una tienda bastante pequeña, donde se venden comestibles
8. Construcción hecha con materiales resistentes, destinada a vivienda o a otros usos
9. Una institución donde se imparte la enseñanza superior
13. Una iglesia grande es una
14. Una persona deposita y retira dinero en un
15. Una obra arquitectónica en memoria a un personaje o un acontecimiento histórico

Down

1. La oficina cuya función es el transporte de la correspondencia
2. Un lugar donde hay operaciones de compra y venta
4. Un lugar donde se elaboran determinados productos
5. Los aviones despegan y aterrizan en el
6. Un templo cristiano es una
10. Un lugar público donde hay competiciones deportivas
11. Un lugar donde se venden productos de toda clase
12. Un lugar ancho y espacioso dentro de una ciudad

Puzzle #82: Current Events/*Temas de Actualidad*

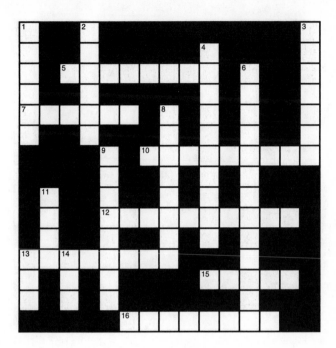

Across

5. The things people are allowed to do
7. Physical or mental strain
10. The opposite of "despair"
12. The acts of selecting leaders
13. The study of government
15. Granting refuge or sanctuary
16. This runs the country

Down

1. Acts against the law
2. The opposite of "peace"
3. Lack of money
4. ___ *médica* (health care)
6. Smog, for example
8. The administration of law
9. The power to act and speak without restraints
11. In a democracy, people get to cast this for their favorite candidate
13. The opposite of "war"
14. A rule of the government

Puzzle #83: Taking Care of Business/*Haciendo Negocios*

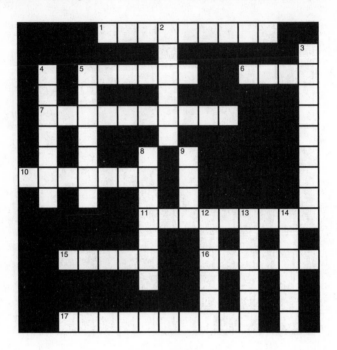

Across

1. What you own
5. To offer something up for sale
6. The total amount
7. The person who uses goods and services
10. Borrowing power
11. Things that are made
15. *Contrato de* ___ (receipt you get at the end of a transaction)
16. Sufficient property to pay debts and legacies
17. Condition when you don't have enough money to pay your bills

Down

2. How much you have to pay
3. Net proceeds
4. Amount due is shown on this
5. Overdue, expired
8. Another way to say "purchase"
9. What you pay each month
12. Opposite of "credit"
13. People set up one of these in a bank
14. The economy is based on ___ and demand

Puzzle #84: Tell It to the Judge/*Dígaselo al Juez*

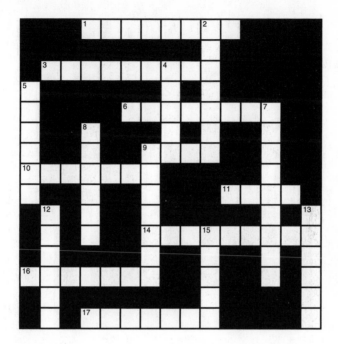

Across

1. Where a trial takes place
3. Guilty or not guilty
6. A person who is found guilty
9. Collective arguments against the accused
10. A court proceeding where a person requests legal remedy
11. The person in charge of the courtroom
14. The opposite of "guilt"
16. The person being defended
17. A person who observed the alleged crime

Down

2. A person who defends or prosecutes
4. Where a prisoner serves time
5. Twelve people listening to a case
7. Facts in the case
8. What you pay so you don't have to stay in jail
9. A punishment or penalty
12. The legal proceeding
13. Another word for "prison"
15. What the defendant is accused of doing

Puzzle #85: Using Analogies/*Usando Analogías*

Across

1. Tenis:cancha :: golf:___
3. Uno:dos :: primero:___
4. Enero:mes :: lunes:___
8. Acabar:terminar :: limpiar:___
9. Pequeño:grande :: estrecho:___
11. Empezar:terminar :: tomar:___
12. Tristeza:melancolía :: felicidad:___
14. Zapatos:pies :: guantes:___
17. Mañana:hoy :: hoy:___
21. Ligero:pesado :: vació:___
22. Suegro:suegra :: yerno:___
23. Antes:después :: desde:___

Down

1. Sí:no :: por:___
2. Nublado:tiempo :: medianoche: ___
3. Mas:menos :: con:___
5. Nunca:siempre :: nada:___
6. Árbol:bosque :: flor:___
7. Encima:debajo :: delante:___
10. Camino:ruta :: autopista:___
13. A la izquierda:a la derecha :: arriba:___
15. Ningún:algún :: nadie:___
16. Rectificar:corregir :: regresar: ___
18. Él:ella :: ellos:___
19. Desear:querer :: permitir:___
20. Vida:muerte :: comienzo:___

Puzzle #86: Using Sports Fields and Equipment/ Usando Los Campos y el Equipo

Across

1. Cuando juego al béisbol, le pego a la pelota con un ___
3. Los jugadores de fútbol americano lanzan un ___
4. Juegan al fútbol en un ___
7. Juego tenis en una ___
8. Para jugar al voleibol, necesito un balón y una ___
10. Necesito una ___ para jugar al jai alai
13. Troto en el ___
14. Cuando voy a la ___, nado en el océano
15. En el invierno, cuando hace mucho frío, juego al baloncesto en un ___

Down

1. Para hacer el ciclismo necesito una ___
2. Patino en una ___
3. Juego a los bolos en una ___
5. Un ___ es una plancha circular que necesitan los jugadores de jockey
6. Las ___ protegen las rodillas
9. Cuando juego al tenis, le pego a la pelota con una ___
10. Cuando hace demasiado frío, nado en una ___ cubierta
11. Cuando juego al jai alai, el ___ es la pared principal
12. Juego al golf en un ___ de golf
16. Buceo en el ___

Puzzle #87: Using Idioms/*Usando Modismos*

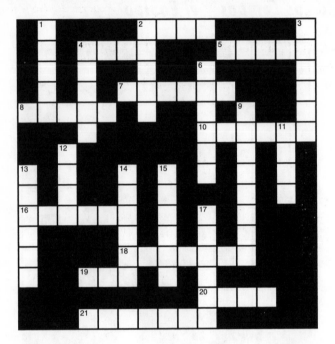

Across

2. *Empezar de* ___ (to start from scratch)

4. *Amargar la* ___ *a alguien* (to make someone's life miserable)

5. *Decir cuatro* ___ (to give someone a piece of one's mind)

7. ___ *a moco tendido* (to cry one's eyes out)

8. *Tocar* ___ (to hit rock bottom)

10. *Tirar la* ___ (to throw in the towel)

16. *Pagar alguien con la misma* ___ (to give someone a taste of his own medicine)

18. *Coger el toro por los* ___ (to take the bull by the horns)

19. *Valer su peso en* ___ (to be worth one's weight in gold)

20. *Estar como pez en el* ___ (to feel completely at home)

21. *Crispar los* ___ (to get on someone's nerves)

Down

1. *Trabajar como un* ___ (to work like a dog)

2. *Echar un* ___ (to give someone a helping hand)

3. *Crecer como la* ___ (to mushroom)

4. *Estar* ___ *de envidia* (to turn green with envy)

6. ___ *las cuarenta* (to give someone a piece of one's mind)

Down (continued)

9. *Acostarse con las* ___ (to go to bed early)

11. *Examinar con una* ___ (to go over with a fine-toothed comb)

12. *Vivir a todo* ___ (to live in style)

13. *Tener un* ___ *de lobo* (to be very hungry)

14. *Pasar la noche en* ___ (to have a sleepless night)

15. ___ *los estribos* (to lose one's temper)

17. *Leer entre* ___ (to read between the lines)

Puzzle #88: What Are You Like?/¿Cómo Es Usted?

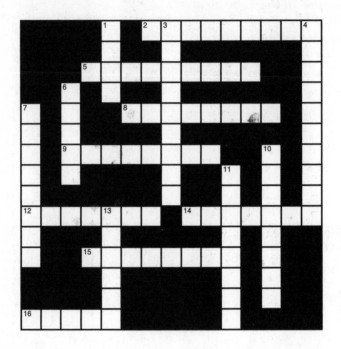

Across

2. Alguien alegre, festivo y de buen humor es ___

5. Alguien que tiene ingenio agudo y penetrante es ___

8. Alguien que no tiene miedo de nada es ___

9. Alguien a quien le gustan los deportes es ___

12. Alguien que olvida los beneficios recibidos es ___

14. Alguien que siempre dice la verdad es ___

15. Alguien que habla mucho es ___

16. Alguien que se mueve con dificultad y que se cae mucho es ___

Down

1. Alguien que traiciona la confianza depositada en el no es ___

3. Alguien que suele hablar o proceder sin reflexión es ___

4. Alguien que olvida las cosas frecuentemente es ___

6. Alguien astuto y prudente es ___

7. Alguien que tiende a la violencia es ___

10. Alguien a quien no le gusta trabajar es ___

11. Alguien magnánimo es ___

13. Alguien digno de ser amado es ___

Puzzle #89: Calculating/*Calculando*

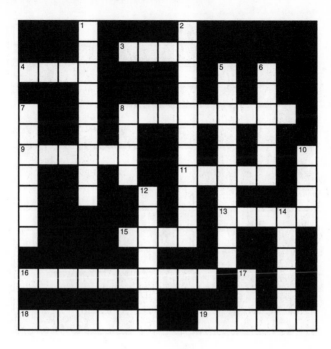

Across

3. Tres por cuatro son ___
4. Setenta y tres y veintisiete son ___
8. Sesenta y cuatro dividido por cuatro son ___
9. Cuatro multiplicado por cinco son ___
11. Tres cuadrado es ___
13. Sesenta y cinco dividido por cinco son ___
15. La raíz cuadrada de treinta y seis es ___
16. Dos mil dividido por cuatro son ___
18. Cuatrocientos sesenta y uno menos trescientos setenta y nueve son ___ y dos
19. Cien mil por diez son un ___

Down

1. Diecisiete multiplicado por tres son ___ y uno
2. Cuatrocientos diecisiete y doscientos ochenta y tres son ___
5. Seiscientos multiplicado por dos son mil ___
6. Ciento treinta y cinco dividido por nueve son ___
7. Setenta y cuatro y diecinueve son ___ y tres
8. La raíz cuadrada de cien es ___
10. Seis y cinco son ___
12. Mil doscientos veinte menos trescientos noventa son ochocientos ___
14. Doscientos cuadrado son ___ mil
17. Tres mil ciento cincuenta y ocho y mil ochocientos cuarenta y dos son cinco ___

Puzzle #90: What Do You Do?/¿Qué Hace Usted?

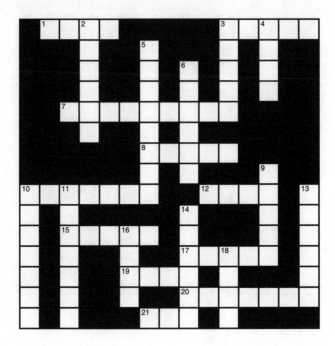

Across

1. Yo ___ el violín en una orquesta
3. Yo ___ mis llaves cuando no puedo encontrarlas
7. Yo ___ en voz alta cada palabra de la frase
8. Yo ___ en coro
10. Yo ___ al profesor cuando el habla
12. Yo ___ en la piscina
15. Yo ___ un traje de baño cuando voy a la playa
17. Yo ___ las notas que están en la pizarra
19. Yo ___ un vaso de agua cuando tengo sed
20. Yo ___ a casa a eso de las cuatro, después de mis clases
21. Yo ___ un paraguas cuando llueve mucho

Down

2. Yo ___ pan en una panadería
3. Yo ___ la rumba
4. Yo ___ mucho cuando hago ejercicios aeróbicos
5. Yo ___ a fumar porque no es bueno para la salud
6. Yo ___ mi plato favorito para la cena
9. Yo ___ la carne con un cuchillo
10. Yo ___ antes de hacer un examen

Down (continued)

11. Yo ___ mi cumpleaños el once de julio

13. Yo ___ dólares en euros en un banco

14. Yo ___ el árbol de Navidad con una guirnalda

16. Yo ___ cuando hay una elección

18. Yo ___ la cuenta con mi tarjeta de crédito

Puzzle #91: Opposite Things/*Cosas Opuestas*

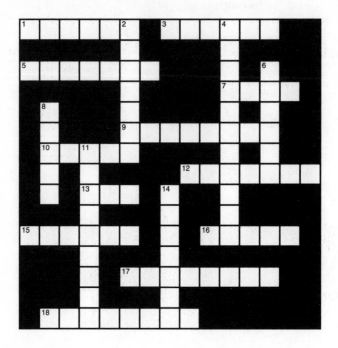

Across

1. Líquido
3. Entrada
5. Amigo
7. Amor
9. Rapidez
10. Tierra
12. Humildad
13. Guerra
15. Nacimiento
16. Tormenta
17. Alegría
18. Fantasía

Down

2. Humildad
4. Insignificancia
6. Campo
8. Mañana
11. Desesperación
14. Verdad

Puzzle #92: Opposite Actions/*Los Acciones Opuestas*

Across

1. Poner
6. Odiar
7. Aumentar
9. Olvidar
10. Renunciar
12. Triunfar
15. Subir
16. Ahorrar
17. Ignorar
18. Abrir
19. Perder

Down

2. Reparar
3. Despedir
4. Recibir
5. Permitir
8. Despertarse
11. Descansar
13. Vender
14. Entrar

Puzzle #93: Repeating the Same Action/ *Repitiendo La Misma Acción*

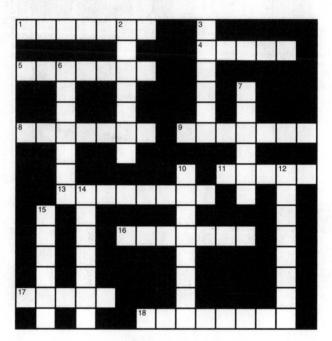

Across

1. Ornamentar
4. Observar
5. Conservar
8. Vacilar
9. Lucir
11. Exigir
13. Venerar
16. Determinar
17. Limpiar
18. Rectificar

Down

2. Inquietar
3. Irritar
6. Adaptar
7. Regresar
10. Acostumbrar
12. Alumbrar
14. Comenzar
15. Notificar

Puzzle #94: What's the Date?/¿Cuál Es la Fecha?

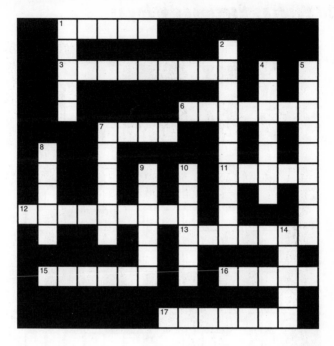

Across

1. Séptimo mes del año
3. Undécimo mes del año
6. Décimo mes del año
7. Quinto mes del año
11. Tercer mes del año
12. Duodécimo mes del año
13. Quinto día de la semana
15. Octavo mes del año
16. Primer día de la semana
17. Séptimo día de la semana

Down

1. Sexto mes del año
2. Noveno mes del año
4. Segundo mes del año
5. Tercer día de la semana
7. Segundo día de la semana
8. Cuarto mes del año
9. Sexto día de la semana
10. Cuarto día de la semana
14. Primer mes del año

Puzzle #95: Wearing Jewels and Jewelry/ *Usando Piedras Preciosas y Joyas*

Across

1. Joya que se lleva en la muñeca y que sirve para marcar la hora
5. Piedra semipreciosa translúcida, opaca y dura, de colores diversos
7. Metal precioso, blanco, brillante e inalterable
8. Anillo de boda
12. Joya que rodea el cuello
13. Piedra preciosa de color verde
16. Joya que se lleva en la oreja
17. Ágata listada de colores alternativamente claros y muy oscuros, que se emplea para hacer camafeos
18. Piedra preciosa de color rojo, correspondiente al mes de febrero
19. Joya (generalmente de metal) que se lleva en el dedo
20. Joya que se lleva prendida en la ropa

Down

1. Piedra preciosa de color rojo, correspondiente al mes de nacimiento de julio

Down (continued)

2. Metal precioso, de color amarillo brillante, dúctil y maleable

3. Piedra muy preciosa, la más dura y brillante

4. Piedra preciosa, amarilla y transparente

6. Materia dura, compacta y blanca

9. Piedra preciosa de color azul verdoso, correspondiente al mes de diciembre

10. Joya formada en el interior de las conchas de diversos moluscos

11. Joya que se lleva en la muñeca

12. Joya formada de una serie de eslabones enlazados, de oro o plata, y que rodea el cuello

14. Joya que se lleva en el dedo y que tiene piedras

15. Piedra preciosa de color azul, correspondiente al mes de septiembre

Puzzle #96: At the Drugstore/*En la Farmacia*

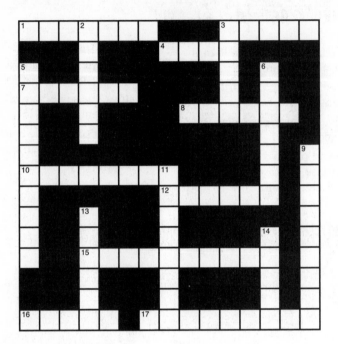

Across

1. *Farmacia de* ___ (a pharmacy that's open all night)
3. Use this for a rash or chafing
4. ___ *de afeitar* (blade that's put in a razor)
7. Use this to look at yourself
8. Use this to wash your hair
10. Medicine in general
12. Use this special pin to secure things
15. Use this to shave
16. Use these drops in your ears
17. Use these drops when you have a cough

Down

2. What the doctor gives for medicine that can't be purchased over the counter
3. ___ *dentrífica*
5. This is used to take your temperature
6. Use it to comb your hair
9. A, B, B_6, B_{12}, C, etc.
11. Pill or capsule taken for body aches
13. Bandage put on a cut
14. *Pañuelos de* ___ (blow your nose in these)

Puzzle #97: School Employees/
Los Empleados de la Escuela

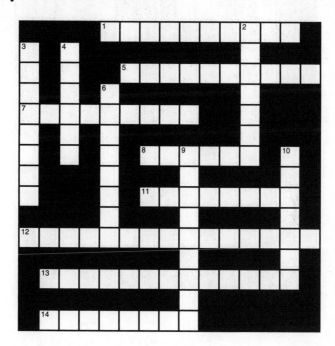

Across

1. Instructor
5. Coach
7. Nurse
8. Dean
11. Janitor
12. Superintendent
13. Librarian
14. Cook

Down

2. *Guardia del ___* (crossing guard)
3. Principal
4. *___ de autobús* (bus driver)
6. Teacher (secondary school)
9. Counselor
10. Teacher (primary school)

Puzzle #98: At College/*En la Universidad*

Across

2. Dormitory
5. Hall
10. Doctorate
11. Office
12. Campus
13. Center
14. Bachelor's degree

Down

1. Laboratory
3. Institute
4. To major
6. To study
7. Library
8. *Estudiante* ___ (graduate student)
9. Course

Puzzle #99: What Do They Do?/*¿Qué Hacen?*

Across

1. Querer tú ___
4. Escoger yo ___
6. Volver él ___
7. Continuar Uds. ___
8. Pensar ellos ___
9. Conducir yo ___
13. Morir ella ___
14. Dirigir yo ___
15. Poder ellos ___
16. Distinguir yo ___
17. Convencer yo ___

Down

2. Enviar tú ___
3. Seguir yo ___
4. Entender Ud. ___
5. Concluir él ___
10. Comenzar tú ___
11. Pedir yo ___
12. Corregir ellos ___
13. Mostrar yo ___

Puzzle #100: On the Table/A la Mesa

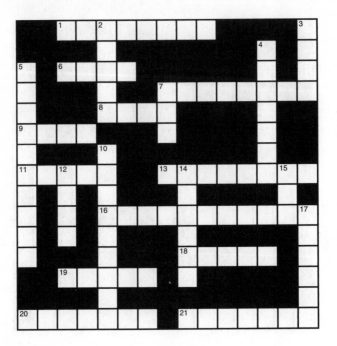

Across

1. Cut your food with this
6. Bees give us this
7. This is often used with salt
8. A clear drink
9. Drink some water out of this
11. Cows give us this
13. Mix this with canned tuna to make salad
16. It's yellow and you put it on bread
18. Put fruit in this
19. Dinner goes on this plate
20. It's yellow and you put it on a hot dog
21. Pick your food with this

Down

2. A very rich addition to coffee
3. Put coffee in this
4. Served on salad with oil
5. Wipe your mouth with this
7. This comes in a loaf
10. You can put this on toast
12. You drink wine out of this
14. Deep-fry in this
15. It often accompanies pepper
17. Use this to make things sweeter

Puzzle #101: Expressing Opinions/*Expresando Opiniones*

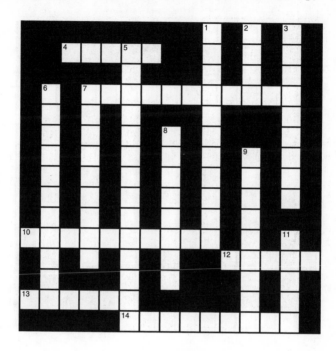

Across

4. Great
7. Scandalous
10. Fantastic
12. Atrocious
13. Super
14. Appalling

Down

1. Wonderful
2. Bad
3. Terrific
5. Incomprehensible
6. Unforgettable
7. Exquisite
8. Boring
9. Ostentatious
11. Silly

Puzzle #102: In the Bookstore/*En la Librería*

Across

1. You'll find dictionaries in this section
3. This section tells you what the future might be like
10. Learn to make paella in this section
11. Keep fit in this part of the bookstore
13. Find classic works like *Don Quijote* here
14. Learn about famous people's lives in this section
15. Make money with books from this part of the store

Down

2. Get swept off your feet here
4. Where you found this book
5. Visit distant lands here
6. Agatha Christie's section of the store
7. A higher power informs this section
8. You'd find one of these in the "books on tape" section
9. Learn about Christopher Columbus here
12. Picasso's area

Appendix A

Solutions to the Easy Puzzles

#1

```
D I R E C C I O N            S A L I R
E           Z            E       O
R U T A     Q            G       T
E       C R U C E        U   O   U
C O M O   I              I   T   L
H       E S Q U I N A    R   R   O
A       S U R            R   E
D           B        U       S   T
    C I U D A D      B   D   E   S
    R       O        U   E       T
H   U   B O C A C A L L E
A   Z       L        A   S   A
C U A D R A R        A   E   N
I   R       R        R   N   T
A           E N F R E N T E
```

#2

```
S I E N T O              V
        O       C   G R I P E
  H U E S O     O       E
        T       N   P   C   R
        O       T   E   U   T
        R   R E S F R I A D O
        N   E   I   O   A   O
    E R U P C I O N     D O L O R
V       D   I   N       E
A S M A R   U       F I E B R E
C       A   P           U
U       R   E   A U X I L I O S
N       A   R           T
A Y U D A R     M E J O R
```

#3

```
          S E G U R O
      R   U         O     T
J E F E   E   P     F     R
  M   F   L   U     I     A
E M P L E A D O     C I T A   B
  R   R   O   S     T   N     J
  E   E   N       J O R N A D A D
  S   N       T       T   N     O
P A R C I A L T U R N O R       R
      I   L       I I           R
    S O L I C I T U D
          B     U
          R   L U G A R
S O B R E S U E L D O
```

#4

```
C I E N   S
      U   I     C U A T R O
    S E S E N T A
      V   T       T E R C E R O
O N C E   E
C           C E R O   D   V
H   D I E Z     C     O   E
E   E       D I E C I S E I S
N   C I N C O     C   N   N
T   M     C   T R E I N T A
A   R T R E S     E     E   E
O         R       U N O
      S E G U N D O   T
          C     O   O C H O
P R I M E R O   S E I S
```

#5

```
C A C A H U E T E
O   E
C I R U E L A   S A N D I A     H
O   E       L           G       A
    E Z     M E L O C O T O N
U V A     P     E           O   R
        P   N U E Z         R   A
P E R A   D     D           O   N
L     S   R     F           N   J
M A N Z A N A   R           J   J
A     O         A V E L L A N A
N           S           I   O
O       F R U T A       M
              A C E I T U N A
```

#6

```
              L
              A         R O S B I F
  T   R       N         A   L
  R   U C     G         L
  U   E E     O         A
  C O R D E R O   A N C H O A
  H   D D     S           H
J A M O N     T           I
              M A R I S C O S
G A M B A S   E   P A T O
      I       S   O   O
  P E S C A D O   O   C
  A   T T       L   I
  V   U U       L   N
  O   C A N G R E J O
              A
```

#7

```
  G R A B A R   E S T I L O
    R                   L
M O S T R A R   C U A D R O
U   E               D   A
R     G E N I O     I   C
A           L       B   U
L     E S C E N A   C   A
I           C       I   R
S   D   E S C U L T U R A
T   E   S   I   J   O   E
A B S T R A C T O       L
    A   U   N   O B R A
    L   E
    L   L U Z
G A L E R I A
```

#8

```
S O M B R A   E X T E R I O R
I   E   A     S           R
S   C M M     A   G       B
T   U R A N O T   A       I
E   R R S     E L U N A   T
M   A I T F   L   A
A   T T L I   I X       C
  C O H E T E R T   B   O
I   E   R T   I   R     M
E   P L A N E T A   I   E
L   L   U B   U     L   T
O   U   T     B     L   A
    T   O     E S T R E L L A
    O             A
    N   G I R A R
```

#9

```
                    B
  P U B L I C O     A
          R   P A P E L
          Q   A   R C O N
    C     U   S   S O     E
T   O     E   I   O   L I N E A S
R A G E   S   L   J         C
A   M     T   L I N E A S   E
G   E D E C O R A D O       N
E   D   A       J         A
D   I   N       T E L O N A
I   A   C       R         I
A C T R I Z   A P L A U D I R
        O         M
A S I E N T O   D I A L O G O
```

#10

```
M   C O N T E S T A R   F
E   U               U
N   E         E S P E R A
S   N   C             R
A L T A V O Z   O C U P A D O
J   A   A           D   I
E     G U I A       D   S
          G       D     C
      C O N T E S T A D O R
      E   U   T
T   L L A M A D A
O   L   U   E   A
N   O   L       N   C O L G A R
O P E R A D O R     I
    R           A
```

#11

#12

#13

#14

#15

#16

#17

#18

#19

#20

#21

#22

#23

#24

#25

#26

#27

```
      P   S
    B O   A       T E R C I O
    O M   C             U
    T R O Z O   B A S T A N T E
    E   L             R
    L I B R A           T A Z A
    L       D E C I M O
  P A Q U E T E           M
  O       A   M E D I O   U
  C A J A     A       P   C
  O     V A S O       I   H
            I   Q U I N T O
    L A T A     N   T
          D O C E N A
      L I T R O
```

#28

```
              I       D I V I D I R
  D E F I N I R       V
  E       T   E       I       D
  C       E   E S C R I B I R E
  I       E   R       R       S
  D E S C R I B I R       C   C
  I       R   I         O   U
  R       U M P       M   B
              R         P   R
  A B R I R   C O M B A T I R
          R   U       R   R
              B       T
  P E R M I T I R   I   P A R T I R
              R
  P R O H I B I R
```

#29

```
  C L A R I N E T E               V
  U   R                           I
  E   P A       S   T E C L A D O O
  R   A         A   R     C       L
  N             X I L O F O N O   O
  O R G A N O   M   P   G   R     N
      R   F     P   G U I D E     C
  T R O M B O N E   U     O       H
      O   N     E   N   F         E
  P I A N O   F L A U T I N       L
      I   F     L       A         O
      C   P A N D E R E T A
      A   U     L       R
        B A T E R I A
              R
              A
```

#30

```
                    I         G
      A L E M A N I A         R E C I A
        B     I   G           E
  D R   R     P O L O N I A   C
  I T A L I A   A   O         I
  N   S       T U R Q U I A   A
  A   I       E     U
  M A R R U E C O S R G U
  A   T U N   E S P A Ñ A     E C
  R   U N   G       S         U C I
  A R G E L I A     U         Z I
      Z   P T   B E L G I C A
        J A P O N   E S T A D O S
```

#31

```
        V E O
        I
    D I C E         E S T A
        N   R E I M O S
        R   I     T I E N E S
        E   E   H A G O     A
            Y         C     L
    P           T R A I G O
    O   S       E   G
  V E N G O     E   G   D O Y
    G   O V A N G O I O
  R I O   O     G     O
        S O Y   O I G O
                    O
```

#32

```
  D   P O R C E N T A J E
  I         E
  V         N   R E S T A R
  I         T         R
  D   M     R E S O L V E R
  C I R C U L O       A   V
  D   L       S   P   L   A
  O   T       R R O   M E N O
  M T R I A N G U L O   E D I R
  E   P       M   R
  N   A L T U R A M E
  O       R     E R E D U C I R
  S O L U C I O N   I   O   N
          A       I O   N O
      P O R               O
```

#33

```
    M A R M O L
    A             L A N A
    D             A     L
  P I E D R A     D     G
    R             R A S O
    P A N A G     I L I N O
    L       A     L     N
    O   C A U C H O
  C O B R E Z   I
  U     M   A E N C A J E
  E   P I E L     R   S
  R     N         C   E
  O   F R A N E L A   D
```

#34

```
          C U I D A D O     Y E S
                            E S O
  R       I R U J         P U L S O
  O       V   J   R       R
  M   V   E   A C C I D E N T E
  P   E   N   N         S       C
  E   N           R A D I O G R A F I A
  N   A           A       T   A M
  S   L   S A L A         A   E I
  E               R           R L
  M U L E T A S       E N F E R M E R A
  E
  S   A U X I L I O S
```

Solutions to the Medium Puzzles

#35

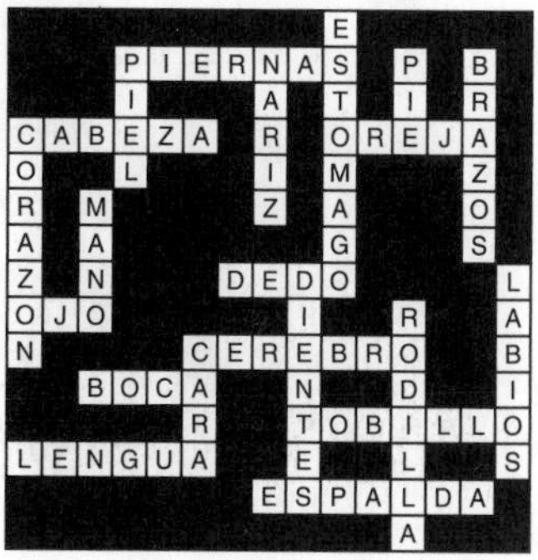

#36

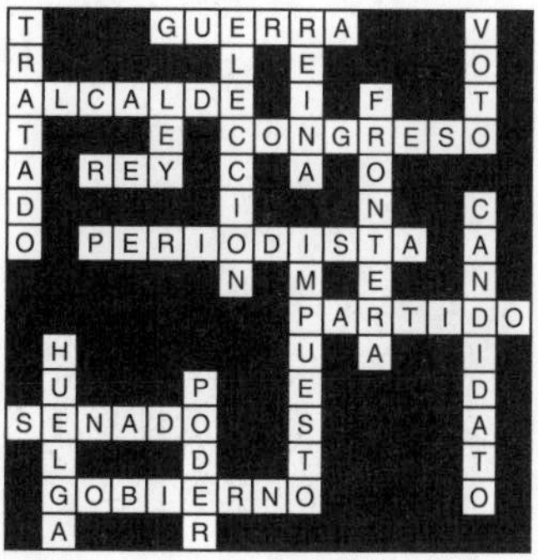

#37

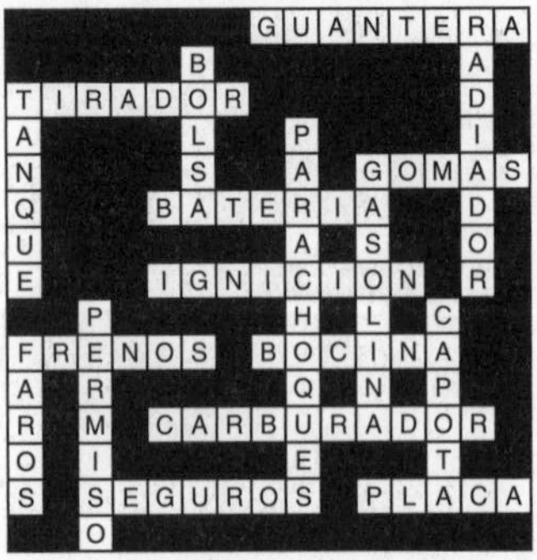

#38

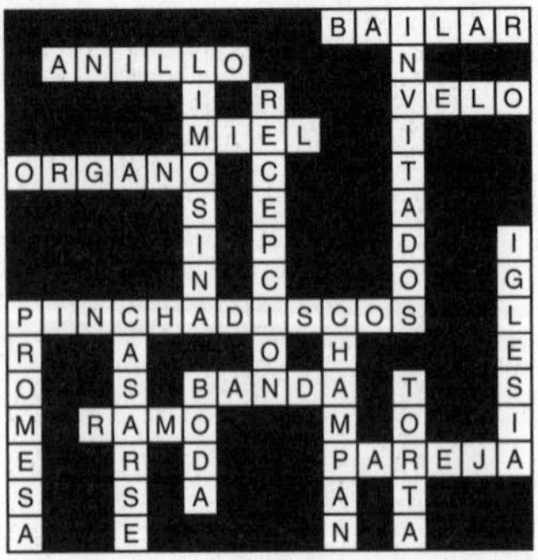

#39

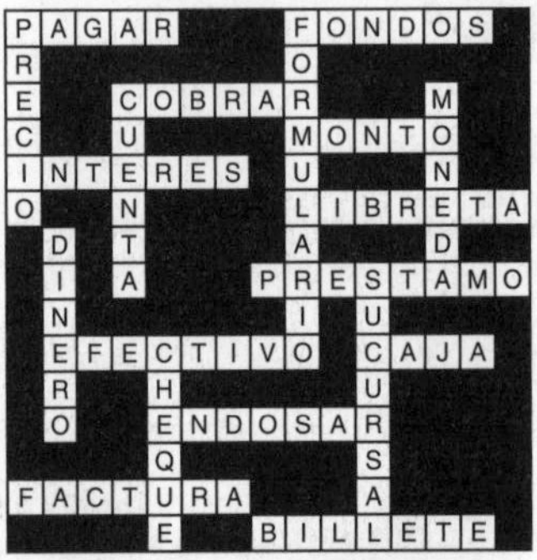

#40

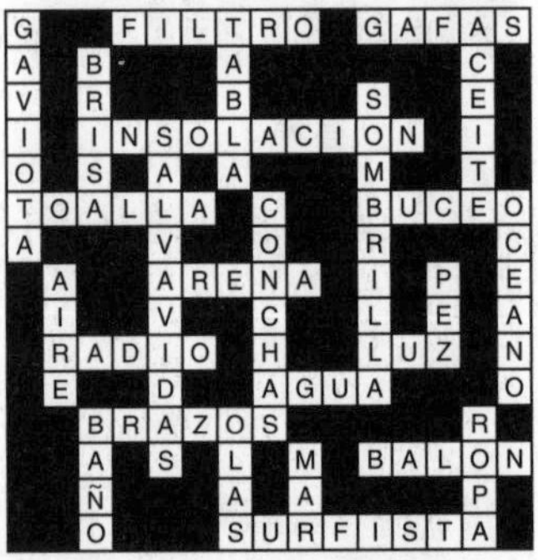

#41

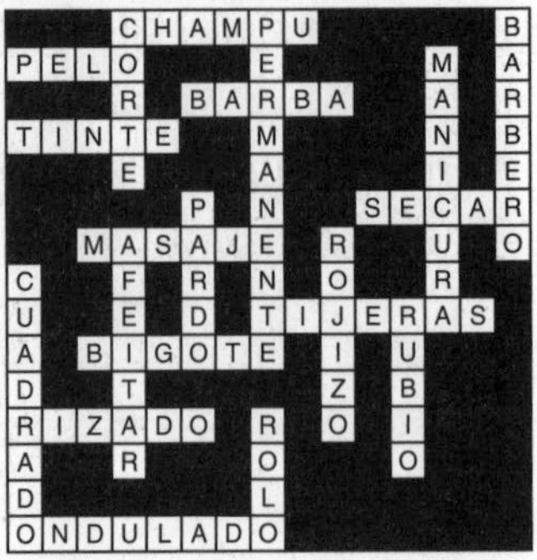

#42

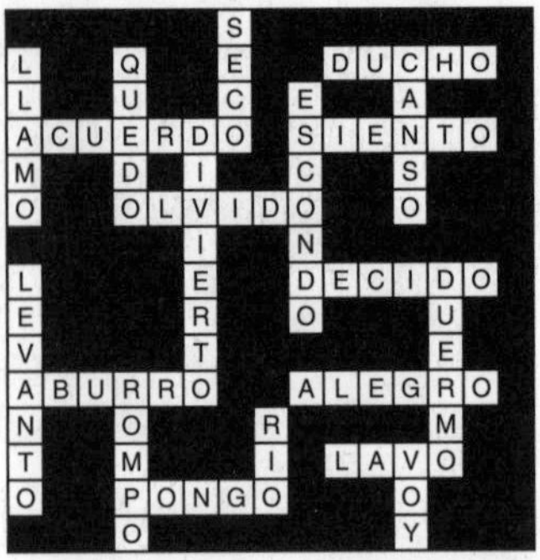

#43

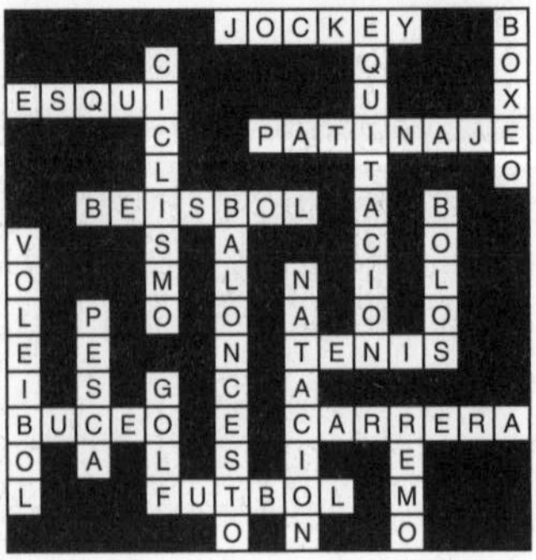

#44

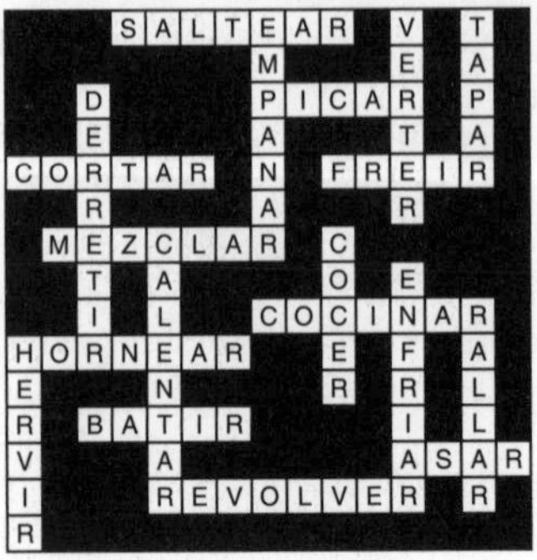

#45

```
      Y               P               T
      E               R               I
      R   M       P   I       H I J O
N I Ñ O   A       I   M       O
I         D       S O B R I N A
E         R       E       M   I
T I A     H E R M A N A   O   V
A   B             N       V   I
    U             E S P O S A
    E             S   A   U
    L             P   D   E
    A B U E L O   R   G
                  S U E G R A
          N I E T O       O
```

#47

```
            Q U E D A
E       A           P R E C I O
E S   A         D   R
T A L L A       E   E
I     M   E     E S T R E C H O
L     A   S     P   A       O
O     C   E     A   D       L
    D E S C U E N T O       G A
      E   A   D   N         U   C
    G R A N D E   L A R G O   S   A
        R     N           U   T   R
      B A R A T O         S
        T     E           T
T A R J E T A   M E D I A N O
```

#49

```
P E P I N O   G       A
I             U       P       P
M       E N D I B I A A       A
I             S   O   P       P
E S P I N A C A       M A I Z
N             N   C       A   A
O   T O M A T E   O       N   N
    C     L   C E B O L L A   A H
    O     E   S   I   B   N   O R
A L C A C H O F A   F A N     R I
    H         N   B R O C O L I A
V E R D U R A     O   R
        G
J U D I A S
```

#51

```
C O M E D O R
U   O             S   G
A R M A R I O   V E N T A N A
R   M             L   R
T   C H I M E N E A   C A S A
O   T           P   O   J
S U E L O       A   C   E
    R           R   I
  P A T I O   S O T A N O
  A   O       A   A
  R   M       M   B
  E   P U E R T A   A
  D E S V A N     T   Ñ
        E S T U D I O
```

#46

```
                              P
            A E R O P U E R T O
E           D           T     R
N           U       A S I E N T O
L L E G A D A       Q       E
A           C O M P A R T I M I E N T O
E           A       A       T       P
        A E R O L I N E A   A       A
            E           O   J       S
            C               E       A
P A S I L L O               T       J
            A       E Q U I P A J E R
V U E L O           D E S T I N O
```

#48

```
C         C O N E X I O N
O         I       R
R         B       R A T O N   U
R         E       O           S
E D E S C A R G A R     P     U
O         E       P A G I N A   R
    C     S       R           I
    A   P A N T A L L A   T   O
M A R C A         T       A
    T   C                     I
    U N I D A D       A       C
    C   O             T E C L A D O
    H O C T E T O     S       N O
```

#50

```
T           T
A       A   I
C O R D O N   E S T U C H E
H       H   T       N       N
U       E   A   S   J       V
E       S   S   U   E   B L O C
L A P I Z   S   J   R       L
A       V   J   E   A       E
S A C A P U N T A S   S     R
        S   A       B       C
P A     G R A P A D O R A   E
A A     O       A       E   S
P L U M A       P           T
E E     A       E           O
L   C A L E N D A R I O
```

#52

```
V I D E O C L U B
            E               J
    C A R N I C E R I A     U
            H           C   G
S U P E R M E R C A D O N   U
      A     R       N   F   E
D     N     I       I   I   T
E     A     A   L   T   T   E
P     D         I   E   E   R
J O Y E R I A   B           I
R     R         R   F L O R E R I A
T     I         E           I
I     A   F R U T E R I A   I
V     O                     I
O         O P T I C A
```

#53

```
T     S U C I O   N
R     E           E
A B U R R I D O   A G R I O
B     I           R     Z
A   F E O   C A R O     Q     A
J   A     C             U     N
A   L E N T O           I     T
D   S     B             E     I
O   O   G R A N D E     R D   P
R       R E           M A L A A
      F   D B           L E T
S A L V A J E   I       L E N O I
  L   I C       L L E N O     I
  T   I         O             C
C O M P L E J O   B A R A T O
```

#54

```
R E C E P C I O N
E       I       H   G
G   D E S P E R T A D O R
A   O           B   B
L               B   E
O           H O S T E R I A
S           A   N
      R   D U C H A N
B O T O N E S   I   N       H
A       S       O   T       U
L       E   M E N S A J E   E
C U B I E R T A     N       S
O N     V       N           P
      C A M A   T           E
            A L M O H A D A
```

#55

```
D         V I E J O
E         D     C   J
L       F R U B I O   O
G     L E     C   M   V
A   L A L     A   P I E L
D E S C U I D A D O   N
O   I Z     C   L       B
      O   C A   X I     E
    G A   A R   I O     L
    U C   T A C I N I C O
A P A R I E N C I A     A
  O   T   N   T   N     L
    U   P E C A S       V
P E S A D O   R   S     O
```

#56

```
C O N C I E R T O       F
    E     E     A       I
P   N     T     A   C I N E S
L   T     U     R       S
A J E D R E Z   R       T
Y   A     O   C O R R I D A
A         R     R       A
        M U S E O       M
        C     I         A
    C   I     C         S
N A I P E S   I     P   B
  R     R     G     A   A
  C A M I N A T A   S   I
  O     M         S E   L
      A T R A C C I O N E S
```

#57

```
                A M A D O
A S U S T A D O L   P
G         N   S I   A
O     A   I   G T   T
T     B   O N E R V I O S O
A     U   T   E   C   O
D   T R I S T E   O     F
    R O   R   C       R
  F U I   O   E       U
  U   D   R   L       S
P R E O C U P A D O   T
  I       D   S E G U R O
S O S P E C H O S O   A
  S                   D
  O       T R A N Q U I L O
```

#58

```
                  S A L
        M         A
        E         B
C R U D O     G   R
        I     R   R
        Z   A S A D O     R
A J O   U   S   S         O
    F   R   A G R I O     M
    U R M   E             E
C O C I D O H   V A P O R O
A   T   S I   U   I       O
R O J O T E   E   C
    P A R R I L L A   N
    Z   B   T         T
E M P A N A D O       E
    S   S   S         E
```

#59

```
D       E S P E R A N Z A
O   U   U
L   F E L I C I D A D
O D I O   U E   E
R   R C E L O S   S     P
    I O   P D   S   E
E   A R   A V E R S I O N A
N   J A   N     E       A
V   A L E M             R
I   L E   I N
D E S E O   N   E N F A D O
I   G     D   D   C
A   O R G U L L O   I
    I         A M O R
D E S A N I M O     N
```

#60

```
    M I S T E R I O
B     N   N       M
I   T E   T       A
L   E   P R O N O S T I C O
L   L   E   O T   Z
E   E   E   V T
T R A N S M I S I O N
E   O   S C I   P   A
    V   I   A   I   N
C O M E D I A A N U N C I O
    L       S   A   I
H O R A R I O     T A M
O   S             A   A
R           A     L   D
A     A V E N T U R A O S
```

#61

```
CHALECO   P
    A      ABRIGO
    M   A N T      B
 VESTIDO  A  CH    U
 C       S  A  H   F
 A     SANDALIAS   A
 L     U    O  Q   N
 C  G  E   CINTURON D
 E  U  T  F    E    A
 T  R  A  A    T
 I  A  J  L BOTAS
 N  N  E  D L
 E  T     VAQUEROS
 S  E     S
 S       ZAPATOS
```

#62

```
      HORQUILLAS
   C            O C
 ESMALTE        C C  G
 P        I     BRILLO
 I        M     O N  M
 L        M        I
DELINEADOR N       N
 L        E        A
PROTECTOR  CREMA
 O        E  J    O
 L        S  O  LAPIZ
 V        O PARPADO E
 O        M     R   I
 S        B    TINTE N
          R       T  E
 MAQUILLAJE
```

#63

```
      R
      O  S      BLANCA
      S  M      R
  CLARO  GRIS   L
      D  R      L    V
   GRANATE      A    E
 A    D         T    R
 MARINO        NEGRO D
 A  A           T    E
 R O JO PASTEL
 I     A        Z
 L  ANARANJADA
 L     D        Z
 O SCURO        U
      VIOLETA
```

#64

```
PSICOLOGO
   O
PLOMERO          E
U   E            N
B   R   PERIODISTA
L   C            R
I   C            E
C  SALVAVIDAS    N
O   N   E    Y   A
   BOTONES   U   D
    E   D    D   O
        EMBAJADOR
        D
        O  CONTABLE
LIBRERO     E
```

#65

```
        BIOLOGIA
   C      R      G
   L   C  Q   M  E
   A  MUSICA  A  O
   S  O   E   T  G
  NEGOCIOS   E  R
   T  T   Q  U  A
 F INFORMATICA  F
 R N      M  T  I
 ALGEBRA  FISICA
 N E      C  C
 CIENCIAS R  A
 E S      R
 S HISTORIA
        E
```

#66

```
PITCHER
R         GUANTE
I     O        R
M  R  JARDINERO
E  E  I   R    O
R  C  T  ARBITRO
BASE      A
A   P  PELOTA   T
T   T      E    E
E   O   JUGADOR
 PARTIDO    D   C
 L      N  CORRER R
 A      R       R A
 T      O
 O  SEGUNDA
```

#67

```
      L
ESTUFA
S  E    V  C  RELOJ
T  L    A  A  E  A
E  E    D  M  F  V
R  V  TOCADOR  I  A
E  I    R    I L  A
O SOFA       G L  S
   O    MOQUETA   P
HORNO        R    I
         SECADORA D
          I   D   O
  CONGELADOR      R
          L       A
BATIDORA
```

#68

```
COMIDA      M
O           O       P
COBIJA      V       A
H    A      I  D    Ñ
E    B   P SILLITA  A
CUENTOS    E    E   L
I    R    R   CUNA
T    O    T        T
O    BACINETE
     B   I
CHUPETE   Ñ
      BIBERON
PELUCHE   R
      SONAJERO
```

Appendix C

Solutions to the Difficult Puzzles

#69

```
      H   ARCE
RAIZ      A            P
O  E  C   CHARCA       I
S  R  O       O        N
A  BARRO  GERANIO
   A   T      T
   T  A VIOLETA
PIEDRA        Z
          TALLO
L             O   L
N    F        RAMA
T    L        O   O
ARBOL         BULBO
         FUENTE   L
```

#70

```
   ARREGLAR        T
D     O    A    E  I
E     T    F  FUNCIONAR
SECO  O    A    I  T
G     S    S  BOTON
A          O    O  R
R          Z       E
REMENDAR        A  R
O          P    B  I
N    LAVANDERIA    I  T
     A     T    I  E
PROBLEMA   R  RELOJ
     A     I       E
           I  VENDER
MANCHA
```

#71
```
E               S
L F CREDITO     O L
E   I           I
C   R           C     B
T O M A R   C   I C   U
R   A     H A B I E N E S C A
I   A     I L     T D     C A R
C       A P R E S T A M O   M
I       N O F A       R M   I
D       U T C A     R
A G E N T E C     B A N C O
D       C C C         I
  C L I M A T I Z A C I O N
      O         O N
  C A S A
```

#72
```
        P
        E       C U R V A
D E R E C H O   E     B
        M   R   L   L L A V E
        I   U   I   O C H     A
M A R   S   C   N   C H       C
    A   O   E   ACCIDENTE     E
C U N E T A         D A       L
    A   M           A         E
    M   A   CONDUCTORA        R
    U   F           N         A
    L   O   ESTACIONAR
    T   O           C
G A T O   REPUESTO
```

#73
```
Q   B             L I M A
U I T O           A     C
I   G         M A N A G U A
T   O         A         P
M O N T E V I D E O     U
      A   A R I D       L
    S A   L E         B C
    A     E           A O
C A N C U N         A R
A   J     C A B O   C E B
R   U     I     L   E   I
A   A     S A N T I A G O L
C   N             P   N B
A           H A B A N A O
S E V I L L A     Z
```

#74
```
B E B I D A         L
A             N U E Z
I       F
L I B R O   P I N T U R A
E       U     A   M     V
        T   S C   B     I N
        C U A R T O     N
            PROFESION    O
M A T E R I A     D      M
            A L   I      B
            L     O M A  R
    P E R I O D I C O    E
    A     Y A     D A
    I             A
P O S T R E   D E P O R T E
```

#75
```
  C   T                 D
  A   R     D I R I G I R
  L A V A R           V
  L   B               I
H A B L A R           D
  R   J A             I
        C O D I A R
S U B I R   B         B
E     H   N O T A R   A
G     T   E   C   J
U S A R   N   O
I     L   S   E X I G I R
R   L E V A N T A R   E
  A         A   M I R A R
T E R M I N A R
```

#76
```
        C A R G O
L U C H A     E
U       L   A V I S O
J       U     I     P
COSTUMBRE     D     R E C
A       N     E     E
MOZO    O   F I N   C
B       L       T   I
O   S A L A M I E D O   G
F   E         I   I     U
U   N   PERSONA   E     S
G   G         I   R     T
RESULTADO     O   I T O
O   A         O
```

#77
```
D R A M A   D     M     N
U     A     E     U     A
L C E S   P E S O E     R
C   C     S   O   O     A
E   A     C U B O T     N
S   A     O               J
F     SURREALISTA         A
U     I             U
E   C D   A C T O R I
NOVELA     O       S
      PORTUGUES    M
  I   I           O
  S   TAPAS   RIO
PAELLA    U
      A L MURALES
```

#78
```
V   E     V A Y A N
U   S       B     E   P
ESCOJAN     R     M   R
L   U       A     P   A
V   CIERREN       I   C
A   H       E   L E   T
N   E       P   L C   I
    N   V   I   E E   Q
        TRAIGAN U   U
MIREN   N   A   U     E
    N   A   PRESTEN
  SIGAN     I   N   S
    A       D       T
  CONTESTEN     N SEAN
```

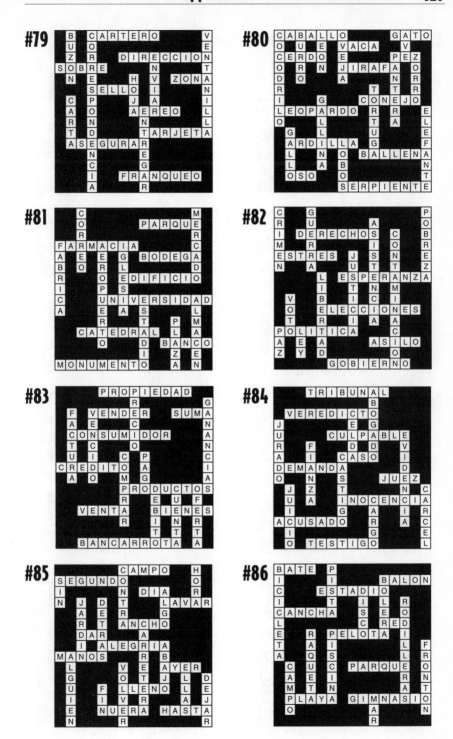

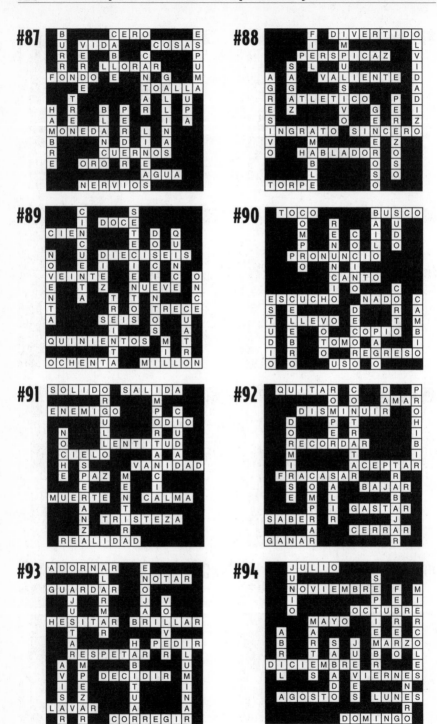

#95

```
        R E L O J
  D   U     R         T
  I   B   O P A L O   M
  A         I     P L A T A
  M     A L I A N Z A   R F
  A           C     I   F U
  N     P P   I   C O L L A R
  T     E U   D     Z   I   Q
  E S M E R A L D A     A   U
  O     R L   S D       F   E
  R     A R E T E       I   S
  T     R     R N       R
O N I C E     A M A T I S T A
  J
  A N I L L O   B R O C H E
```

#96

```
G U A R D I A         P O L V O
        E       H O J A S
  T     C         S       C
T E S P E J O     T       E
R     T           A   C H A M P U
M     A             P   I     V
O                   I   L     I
M E D I C I N A     L   L     T
E       C       S E G U R O   A
T       U       P     O   P   M
R       R       I         P   I
O       R A S U R A D O R A   N
        I       I         P   A
        T       N         E
G O T A S     P A S T I L L A S
```

#97

```
        I N S T R U C T O R
  D C           R
  I H     E N T R E N A D O R
  R O   P       F
  E F E R M E R A   I
  C E   O         C
  T R   F   D E C A N O   M
  O R   E       O       A
  R     S   C O N S E R J E S
        O       S       S
S U P E R I N T E N D E N T E
              J         R
  B I B L I O T E C A R I O
              R
  C O C I N E R O
```

#98

```
        L   D O R M I T O R I O
        A   E     N
        B   S   P A S I L L O
        O   P   T       T
        R   E S T I T U T O   G
  B     A   C   T   C   U     R
  I     T   I   U   U   R     A
  B     O   A   D O C T O R A D O
  L     R   L   I   O   S     U
  I     I     O F I C I N A   A
  O     O       A       O     D
  T         O   Z
  E         A         C A M P O
  C E N T R O     S
  A         L I C E N C I A T U R A
```

#99

```
  Q U I E R E S
      N     I     E S C O J O
V U E L V E G N   O
      I     G C O N T I N U A N
      A     I C   L
P I E N S A N   E   L
            C O N D U Z C O
  P   C     D   Y   O
  I   O     M U E R E M
  D I R I J O   U     S
  O   R     E   P U E D E N
      I     S   E     N
      G   D I S T I N G O Z A
      E     R         A S
C O N V E N Z O
```

#100

```
      C U C H I L L O     T
      R         V I   A Z
S   M I E L     I   V I
E     M       P I M I E N T A
R     A G U A     N A G R
V A S O   N       A G R
I     M           R
L E C H E     M A Y O N E S A
O   R   C       A
E   P   M A N T E Q U I L L A
T   A   E   I         Z
A   L   L   T A Z O N   U
    P L A T O   E       C
    D             A S   A
M O S T A Z A   T E N E D O R
```

#101

```
              M   M   F
    R E G I O A   A   E
        N     R   L   N
    E S C A N D A L O S O
  I N   O   A   V   O M
  N O Q U M   B U   E
  O L U I P R U   M
  L V I S R E R   N
  V I S I R N R   S
  I D I N   R   O T
  D A O     I   S E
F A N T A S T I C O   T
  B L O   I D O   A T R O Z
  L   O   D     O S N
G E N I A L     S   T
        E S P A N T O S O
```

#102

```
      R E F E R E N C I A
            O
            M
  C I E N C I A F I C C I O N
            N   R       V
  M   R   A   C   U   H I
  I   E   U   E   C O C I N A
  S A L U D     A I G   T   J
  T   I   O     R G R   O   E
  E   G   R     T R     R   S
  R   I   L I T E R A T U R A
  I   O   I       M     I
  O   N   B I O G R A F I A
          R       S
  N E G O C I O S
```

Appendix D

Word Finder

a un, una

ability habilidad

abolish (to) abolir

abortion aborto

above encima de

absent ausente

abstract abstracto

absurd absurdo

abuse abuso

accelerate (to) acelerar

accelerator acelerador

accept (to) aceptar

access (to) entrar

accident accidente

according to según

accordion acordeón

account cuenta

accountant contable

across from enfrente de

action acción

activity actividad

actor actor

actress actriz

add (to) añadir, sumar

address dirección

addressee destinatario

adhesive tape cinta adhesiva

administration administración

administrator administrador(a)

admissions admisiones

admit (to) admitir

adventure aventura

adventuresome aventurero(a)

advisable conviene

aerobics aeróbicos

affectionate cariñoso(a),

afectuoso(a)

affirm afirmar

African africano(a)

African American afroamericano(a)

after después, tras

afternoon tarde

afterward después

again de nuevo

against contra

agent agente

aggressive agresivo(a)

ago hace

aide ayudante

aim propósito

air aire

air conditioner acondicionador de aire

air letter aerograma

air-conditioned climatizado

air-conditioning climatización

airbag bolsa de aire

airline aerolínea

airmail correo aéreo

airplane avión

airport aeropuerto

aisle pasillo

alarm clock despertador

algebra álgebra

Algeria Argelia

all-night pharmacy farmacia de guardia

allow (to) dejar

almond almendra

almost casi

also también

alteration alteración

always siempre

amazing asombroso(a)

ambassador embajador(a)

American estadounidense

amethyst amatista

among entre

amount cantidad

amuse (to) divertir

amusement park parque de atracciones

amusing divertido(a)

anchovy anchoa

anger enfado

animal animal

ankle tobillo

answer respuesta

answer (to) contestar

answering machine contestador automático

antacid antiácido

anticipation expectación

antihistamine antihistamínico

antiseptic antiséptico

anxiety inquietud

anxious ansioso(a)

apartment apartamento

apathetic apático(a)

appalling espantoso(a)

appearance apariencia

appetizer aperitivo

applaud (to) aplaudir

apple manzana

appliance store tienda de aparatos electrodomésticos

apply for (to) solicitar

apply makeup (to) pintarse, maquillarse

appointment cita

apprehend (to) aprehender

apricot albaricoque

April abril

aquamarine aguamarina

aquarium acuario

Arab árabe

architect arquitecto(a)

area área

area code código de área

arena arena

arm brazo

armchair sillón

around alrededor de

arrival llegada

arrive (to) llegar

art arte

art gallery galería de arte

artichoke alcachofa

articles artículos

artificial artificial

artist artista

arts letras

arts and crafts artesanía

arts and crafts store tienda de artesanías

as tan

as soon as possible cuanto antes

ashamed avergonzado(a)

ashtray cenicero

Asian asiático(a)

ask (to) preguntar, pedir

asparagus espárragos

aspirin aspirina

assets bienes

assistant asistente, ayudante

assistant manager subgerente

asteroid asteroide

asthma asma

astronaut astronauta

asylum asilo

at about a eso de

at the bottom of en el fondo de

at the end of al final de

at the foot of al pie de

at the side of al lado de

at the top of en lo alto de

athlete atleta

athletic atlético

athletics atletismo

atmosphere atmósfera

atrocious atroz

attend (to) asistir

attic desván, ático, entretecho

attitude actitud

attract (to)   atraer

auburn   rojizo

audience   público

auditorium   auditorio

August   agosto

aunt   tía

Australian   australiano(a)

authentic   auténtico

author   autor

authorize (to)   autorizar

autumn   otoño

avenue   avenida

average   promedio

aversion   aversión

avocado   aguacate

avoid (to)   evadir

awesome   bárbaro(a)

baby tooth   diente de leche

baby-sitter   niñera

Bachelor's degree   licenciatura

back   espalda

backpack   mochila

backyard   patio

bacon   tocino

bad   malo(a)

bag   saco

baggage   equipaje

baggage claim   reclamo de equipaje

baggy   holgado(a)

bail   fianza

bake (to)   hornear

baked   asado

baker   panadero(a)

bakery   panadería

balance   saldo

balcony   balcón

bald   calvo(a)

ball   pelota, balón

ballet   ballet

balloon   globo

ballpoint pen   bolígrafo

banana   banana

band   banda

bandage   venda

band-aid   curita

bangs   flequillo

bank   banco

bank book   libreta

banker   banquero(a)

bankruptcy   bancarrota

bar   tableta, barra

barbecue grill   parrilla

barber   barbero

bark   corteza

base   base

base (first)   primera

base (second)   segunda

base (third)   tercera

baseball   béisbol

basement   sótano

basil   albahaca

basketball baloncesto

bass merluza

bassinet bacinete

bassoon fagot

bat bate

bathe (to) bañarse

bathing suit traje de baño

bathroom baño

bathtub bañera

batter (baseball) bateador

battery batería

bay leaf hoja de laurel

be (permanent condition) (to) ser

be (temporary condition) (to) estar

be able to (to) poder

be bored stiff (to) aburrirse como una ostra

be born (to) nacer

be cold (to) hace frío

be cool (to) hace fresco

be crazy about (to) estar bobo(a)

be fed up (to) estar hasta el gorro

be glad (to) alegrarse

be green with envy (to) estar verde de envidia

be hot (to) hace calor

be in on the secret (to) estar en el ajo

be madly in love (to) estar colado

be missing (to) faltar

be mistaken (to) equivocarse

be named (to) llamarse

be on television (person) (to) salir por televisión

be quiet (to) callar

be sunny (to) hace sol

be very hungry (to) tener un hambre de lobo

be windy (to) hace viento

be worth (to) valer

be worth one's weight in gold (to) valer su peso en oro

beach playa

beach chair tumbona

beach towel toalla de playa

beach umbrella sombrilla de playa

beachball balón de playa

beachwear ropa de playa

beans (green) judías

bear oso

beard barba

beat (to) batir

beat around the bush (to) andarse con chiquitas

beautiful bello(a), hermoso(a)

beauty belleza

beauty products productos de belleza

become angry (to) enojarse, enfadarse

become bored (to) aburrirse

become frightened (to) asustarse

become tired (to)   cansarse

bed   cama

bedroom   dormitorio

beef   carne de res

beer   cerveza

beets   remolachas

before   ante

begin (to)   comenzar, empezar

beginning   comienzo

behave (to)   portarse

behind   detrás de, tras

beige   beige

Belgium   Bélgica

bell   timbre

bellhop   botones

below   abajo

belt   cinturón

beneath   debajo de

benefits   beneficios

better   mejor

between   entre

bib   babero

bicycle   bicicleta

big   grande

bill   billete, factura, cuenta

bill of sale   contrato de venta

biology   biología

bird   ave, pájaro

birth   nacimiento

bitter   amargado(a), agrio

black   negro(a)

blackberry   zarzamora

blanket   manta

bleed (to)   sangrar

blender   licuadora

blender, mixer   batidora

block   cuadra

blocks   cubitos

blond (hair)   rubio(a)

blood   sangre

blood pressure   presión arterial

blouse   blusa

blow dry (to)   secar

blue   azul

blueberry   mirtillo

blunt (haircut)   en cuadrado

blush   colorete

board game   juego de mesa

boarding pass   tarjeta de embarque

boat   barco

bobby pins   horquillas

body   cuerpo

body-building   fisiculturismo

boil (egg, vegetables, or meat) (to)   cocer

boil (liquid) (to)   hervir

boiled   cocido

book   libro

bookcase   librero

bookends   sujetalibros

bookkeeper   tenedor(a) de libros

bookkeeping   contabilidad

bookmark marcador

bookmark marca

bookseller librero(a)

bookstore librería

boot (to) arrancar

boots botas

border frontera

bore (to) aburrir

bored aburrido(a)

boredom aburrimiento

boring aburrido(a)

borrow (to) tomar prestado

boss jefe(a)

bottle botella

bottle (baby) biberón

boulevard bulevar

bowl tazón

bowling bolos

bowling alley bolera

box caja

boxing boxeo

boyfriend novio

bracelet pulsera

brain cerebro

brakes frenos

branch (bank) sucursal

branch (tree) rama

brave valiente

Brazil Brasil

Brazilian brasileño(a)

bread pan

bread (to) empanar

breaded empanado(a)

break (to) romper

break (body part) (to) romperse

breakfast desayuno

break-ins robos

breeze brisa

brick ladrillo

bright brillante

bring (to) llevar, traer

broadcast transmisión

broccoli brócoli

broiled a la parrilla

broken bone hueso roto

brook arroyo

brother hermano

brother-in-law cuñado

brown pardo

brown (hair) castaño

browse (to) echar una ojeada

bruise contusión

brunette castaño

brush cepillo

brush hair (to) cepillarse

brussels sprouts bretones

buckle (to) abrocharse

bud botón

Buddhist budista

budget presupuesto

bug error

build (physique) complexión

building edificio

bulb bulbo

bull toro

bullfight corrida de toros

bump hinchazón

bumper parachoques

burglar alarm alarma antirrobo

burn quemadura

bursar tesorero

bus autobús

bus driver chofer de autobús

bush arbusto

business comercio, negocio

business center centro de negocios

businessperson comerciante

busy ocupado(a)

butcher carnicero(a)

butcher shop carnicería

butter mantequilla

button botón

buy (to) comprar

buyer comprador(a)

byte octeto

cabbage col

cable television televisión por cable

cactus cacto

cafeteria cafetería

cake pastel, torta

calculate (to) calcular

calculator calculadora

calendar calendario

calf pantorrilla

call llamada

call (to) llamar

call waiting llamada en espera

caller ID identificación de llamada

calm tranquilo(a), calma

calm (to) calmar, tranquilizar

camera cámara

camera shop tienda de fotografía

campus campo

can lata

can opener abrelatas

Canadian canadiense

candid cándido(a)

candidate candidato

candy dulces

candy store confitería

cane bastón

canoe canoa

canoeing piragüismo

cap gorra de béisbol

capable capaz

caper alcaparrón, alcaparra

capital capital

capture (to) capturar

car automóvil, coche, carro

car rental alquiler de carros

carafe garrafa

caramel custard flan

carbon monoxide detector
detector de monóxido de carbono

carburator carburador

card tarjeta

cards naipes

carnival carnaval

carpenter carpintero(a)

carpet moqueta

carriage (baby) cochecito

carrier (baby) portabebés

carrot zanahoria

carry-on luggage equipaje de mano

cart carrito

cartoon dibujos animados

cartridge cartucho

case caso

cash dinero en efectivo

cash (a check) (to) cobrar

cash register caja

cashier cajero(a)

cashmere cachemira

cast yeso

castanets castañuelas

castle castillo

cat gato

catch (to) coger, atrapar

catcher receptor

cathedral catedral

Catholic católico(a)

cauliflower coliflor

CD player tocador de CD

cedar cedro

ceiling techo

celebrate (to) celebrar

celery apio

cell celda

cell phone teléfono celular

cello violonchelo

cement cemento

center centro

ceremony ceremonia

certain cierto

certainty certeza

certified mail correo certificado, recomendado

chain cadena

chair silla

chalk tiza

chalkboard pizarra

champagne champaña

championship campeonato

change (clothing) cambiarse

change (money) cambio

change (to) cambiar

changeable inestable

character carácter, personaje

characterize (to) caracterizar

charge cargo

chat (to) charlar, platicar

cheap barato

check (money) cheque

checkbook chequera

checkers damas

cheek   mejilla

cheese   queso

chemistry   química

cherry   cereza

chess   ajedrez

chest   pecho

chestnut   castaña, marrón

chestnut brown   pardo

chicken   pollo

child   chico, niño

childish   infantil

chill (to)   enfriar

chills   escalofrío

chin   barbilla

Chinese   chino(a)

chives   cebollina

chocolate shop   chocolatería

choose (to)   escoger, optar

chop (to)   picar

chorus   coro

church   iglesia

cider   sidra

circle   círculo

circumference   circunferencia

circus   circo

city   ciudad

civil-service worker   empleado público

civilizations   civilizaciones

clam   almeja

clarinet   clarinete

class   clase

classified ads   anuncios clasificados

classify (to)   clasificar

classroom   aula, salón

clay   arcilla

clean   limpio(a)

clean (to)   limpiar

clear   claro

clerk   dependiente

click (to)   chascar

climate   clima

clip   pinza

clipboard   tabloncillo

clock   reloj

close (an account) (to)   liquidar

close (to)   cerrar

closed   cerrado(a)

closet   armario

clothes (baby)   ropita

clothing   ropa

clothing store   tienda de ropa

cloud   nube

cloudy   nublado(a)

club   círculo

clumsy   torpe

clutch pedal   embrague

coach (trainer)   entrenador(a)

coast   costa

coat   abrigo

coconut   coco

COD (collect on delivery)   contra reembolso

codfish bacalao

coffee café

coffeemaker cafetera

coin moneda

cold resfriado

colleague colega

collect call llamada por cobrar

collection colección

collide (to) chocar

cologne agua de Colonia

color color

coloring tinte

coloring book librito de colorear

comb peine

comb hair (to) peinarse

combat combate

combine (to) combinar

come (to) venir

comedy comedia

comet cometa

comical cómico(a)

commercial anuncio

commercial break pausa comercial

commission comisión

common usual

company empresa, compañía

compare (to) comparar

compartment compartimiento

competition competición

competitor competidor

complain (to) quejarse

complex complejo

complicate matters (to) buscarle cinco patas al gato

complicated complicado(a)

computer ordenador, computadora

computer science informática

computer store tienda de ordenadores (computadoras)

concert concierto

concierge conserje

conclude (to) concluir

conclusion conclusión

condominium condominio

cone cono

confident seguro(a)

confused confundido(a)

congress congreso

connection conexión

connection enlace

consequence consequencia

consequently por consiguiente

consist (to) consistir

constellation constelación

consult (to) consultar

consultant consultor(a)

consume (to) consumir

consumer consumidor

contact lens lentilla de contacto

contemplate (to) contemplar

contempt desdén

continue (to) seguir, continuar

contract   contrato

converse (to)   conversar

convince (to)   convencer

cook   cocinero(a)

cook (to)   cocinar

cookie   galletita

cooler   nevera portátil

copper   cobre

copy (to)   copiar

cordless phone   teléfono inalámbrico

corduroy   pana

corn   maíz

corner   esquina

correct (to)   corregir

correction fluid   corrector

correspondence   correspondencia

cost   costo

cost (to)   costar

Costa Rican   costarricense

cotton   algodón hidrófilo

cough   tos

counselor (adviser)   consejero(a)

count (to)   contar

counter   mostrador

countertop oven   horno de encimera

country   país, campo

coup   golpe

courage   coraje

course   campo, curso

court   tribunal

court (tennis)   cancha

courteous   cortés

courtyard   patio

cousin   primo(a)

cover (baby)   cobija

cover (to)   cubrir, tapar

cow   vaca

coward   cobarde

cowardly   cobarde

CPU   unidad central

crab   cangrejo

cracker   galleta

cradle   cuna

cranberry   arándano

crayons   lápices para pintar

cream   crema

credit   crédito

credit card   tarjeta de crédito

crew   tripulación

crime   crimen

critic (reviewer)   crítico(a)

crocodile   cocodrilo

cross (to)   cruzar

crossing   cruce

crossing guard   guardia del tráfico

crossword puzzle   crucigrama

cruise   crucero

crutches   muletas

cry (to)   llorar

cry one's eyes out (to)   llorar a moco tendido

cucumber   pepino

culture cultura

cup taza

curb cuneta

cure cura

curious curioso(a)

curl (to) rizar

curly rizado(a)

currant grosella

curtain telón

curtains cortinas

curve curva

custom costumbre

customs aduana

cut corte

cut (to) cortar

cut oneself (to) cortarse

cyberspace ciberespacio

cycling ciclismo

cylinder cilindro

cynical cínico(a)

dairy products productos lácteos

dairy store lechería

damages daños

dance baile

dance (to) bailar

dandruff caspa

dare atrevarse

dark oscuro(a)

database base de datos

date dátil

daughter hija

daughter-in-law nuera

day día

day off día libre

dean decano

death muerte

debit débito

December diciembre

decide (to) decidir

declare (to) declarar

decorate (to) decorar

defendant acusado(a)

defense defensa

define (to) definir

definition definición

degree grado, título

dejection desánimo

delete (to) borrar

delicatessen salchichonería

deliver (to) entregar, repartir

delivery man (woman) repartidor(a)

demand (to) exigir, demandar

democracy democracia

den estudio

denim la tela vaquera

Denmark Dinamarca

dentist dentista

deny (to) negar

deodorant desodorante

department departamento

department store almacén

departure salida

deposit depósito

deposit (to) depositar, ingresar

depressed deprimido(a)

descend (to) descender

describe (to) describir

desert desierto

designer diseñador(a)

desire deseo

desire (to) desear

despair desesperación

dessert postre

destination destino

detail detalle

detest (to) detestar

diagram diagrama

dial disco

dial (to) marcar

dial tone tono, señal

dialogue diálogo

diameter diámetro

diamond diamante

diaper pañal

dice (to) picar

dictator dictador(a)

dictionary diccionario

die (to) morir

difficult difícil

digit dígito

digital digital

dill eneldo

diminish (to) disminuir

dining room comedor

dinner cena

dinner plate plato

diploma diploma

direct (to) dirigir

direction dirección, sentido

directional signal señal direccional

dirty sucio

discipline disciplina

discount descuento, rebaja

discourteous descortés

discover (to) descubrir

discoverer descubridor

discuss (to) discutir

disgust indignación, repugnancia

disgusting asqueroso(a)

dish plato

dishonor deshonor

dishwasher lavaplatos

disk drive disquetera

dissolve (to) disolver

distance distancia

distinguish (to) distinguir

distinguish right from wrong (to) distinguir lo blanco de lo negro

distress angustia

divide (to) dividir, partir

divided by dividido por

divider separador

diving buceo

dizziness vértigo

dizzy mareado(a)

do (to) hacer

doctor médico, doctor

doctor's office consultorio

doctorate doctorado

document documento

documentary documental

dog perro

doll muñeca

dolphin delfín

domicile domicilio

donkey burro

door puerta

door handle tirador de la puerta

doorman portero

dormitory dormitorio

doubt duda

doubtful dudoso

down payment desembolso inicial

download (to) descargar

downpour aguacero

dozen docena

drama drama

dramatist dramaturgo(a)

drawing dibujo, diseño

dress vestido

dresser tocador, cómoda

dressing vendaje

dressmaker costurera, modista

drink bebida

drive (to) dirigir, conducir

driver conductor (conductora), chofer

driver's license permiso de conducir

drop gota

drop (to) dejar

drops (cough) pastillas

drops (eye or ear) gotas

drugs drogas

drugstore farmacia

drum tambor

drumset batería

dry seco(a)

dry (to) secar

dry clean lavar en seco

dry cleaner's tintorería

dry myself (to) secarse

dryer secadora

dubbed versión doblada

duck pato

due vencido(a)

dull opaco

during durante

dust polvo

Dutch holandés (holandesa)

dye tinte

e-mail correo electrónico

ear oreja

early temprano

earn (to) ganar

earring arete

earth tierra

east este

easy fácil

eat like a pig (to) comer como un cerdo

eat lunch (to) almorzar

eclipse eclipse

economy economía

editor redactor(a)

education educación

effect efecto

eggplant berenjena

eggs huevos

Egypt Egipto

eight ocho

eighteen dieciocho

eighth octavo

eighty ochenta

elation euforia

elbow codo

election elección

electric adapter transformador

electrician electricista

electricity electricidad

electronics store tienda de aparatos electrónicos

elegant elegante

elephant elefante

elevator ascensor

eleven once

elm olmo

embassy embajada

emerald esmeralda

emergency exit salida de emergencia

emergency room sala de emergencias

emotion emoción

employee empleado(a)

empty vacío(a)

empty (to) vaciar

end fin

endive endibia

endorse (to) endosar

enemy enemigo

engineer ingeniero(a)

England Inglaterra

English inglés (inglesa)

engraving grabado

enjoy (to) gozar

enough suficiente, bastante

enter (to) entrar, pasar

entrance entrada

envelope sobre

envy envidia

equality igualdad

equation ecuación

era era

erase (to) borrar

eraser goma

error error, falta

escalator escalera eléctrica

escape (to) escaparse

espionage, spy espionaje

essential esencial

etch (to) grabar

etching aguafuerte

euro euro

Europe Europa

European europeo(a)

eve víspera

evidence (proof) evidencia

evident evidente

exact exacto

exactly en punto

example ejemplo

exceed (to) exceder

excellent excelente

excessively demasiado

exchange rate el tipo de cambio

excited emocionado(a)

excuse (to) excusar, perdonar

exercise ejercicio

exhausted agotado(a)

exhaustion fatiga

exhibit (to) exhibir

exist (to) existir

exit salida

exit (to) salir

expenses gastos

expensive caro(a)

experience experiencia

expert experto(a)

explain (to) explicar

explanation explicación

explore (to) explorar

export (to) exportar

expression expresión

exquisite exquisito(a)

extraordinary extraordinario(a)

eye ojo

eye shadow sombra de ojos

eyebrow ceja

eyeglasses gafas, lentes

eyelash pestaña

eyelid párpado

eyeliner delineador de ojos

face cara

facial masaje facial

factory fábrica

facts hechos

fail (to) fracasar

fair feria, justo

faithful fiel

fake falso

fall (to) caer(se)

fall asleep (to) dormirse

famous famoso(a)

fan ventilador

fantastic fantástico(a)

fantasy fantasía

far lejos

farmer campesino(a)

fast rápido

fat grasa, gordo(a)

father padre

father-in-law suegro

faucet grifo, llave

fear miedo, temor

February febrero

feel (to) sentarse

feel completely at home (to)
estar como pez en el agua

fencing esgrima

fender guardafango

fennel hinojo

fever fiebre

few poco(a)

fiber fibra

field campo

fifteen quince

fifth quinto

fifty cincuenta

fig higo

fight (to) luchar, pelear, combatir

file cabinet fichero

fill (out) (to) llenar

film película

filter filtro

finally al fin

find (to) hallar, encontrar

fine multa

finger dedo

finish (to) terminar, acabar

Finland Finlandia

fire fuego, incendio

fire (to) despedir

firefighter bombero(a)

fireplace chimenea

first primero

first aid primeros auxilios

fish pescado

fish (alive) pez

fish store pescadería

fishing pesca

fit (to) quedar, caber

fitness center gimnasio

fitting conveniente

five cinco

five hundred quinientos

fix (to) arreglar

flannel franela

flavoring esencia

fleet flota

flight vuelo

floor suelo

floor (story) piso

florist florería

flounder platija

flower flor

flower shop florería

flu gripe

flute flauta

fly (a kite) volar

foam espuma

fog niebla

folder carpeta

foliage follaje

follow (to) seguir

food alimento, comestible, comida

food processor procesador de alimentos

foot pie

for (in order to) para

for (on behalf of) por

forbid (to) prohibir

forecast pronóstico meteo-rológico

forehead frente

foreign trade comercio exterior

forest selva

forget (to) olvidar(se)

forgetful olvidadizo

fork tenedor

form formulario

forty cuarenta

foundation base

fountain fuente

four cuatro

fourteen catorce

fourth cuarto

fox zorro

fraction fracción

fragrance fragrancia

France Francia

freckles pecas

free (to) emancipar

freedom libertad

freeze congelar, helar

freezer congelador

French francés (francesa)

Friday viernes

fried frito

friend amigo

friendly amistoso(a)

frightened asustado(a)

from desde

from time to time de vez en cuando, a veces

front frente

frost escarcha

fruit fruta

fruit store frutería

frustrated frustrado(a)

fry (to) freír

frying pan sartén

fulfill (to) cumplir

full lleno(a)

full-time tiempo completo

fun divertido(a)

funds fondos

funny cómico(a)

fur piel

fur store peletería

furious furioso(a)

furniture mueble(s)

furniture store mueblería

gabardine gabardina

galaxy galaxia

gallery galería

game juego

game (meat) caza

game show juego

gangs pandillas

garage garaje

garage-door opener de garajes abridor

garbage collector basurero(a)

garbage disposal triturador de basura

garden jardín

garlic ajo

gas gasolina

gas station gasolinera

gas tank tanque

gate puerta

gear shift cambio de velocidades

gel gomina, gelatina

generous generoso(a)

genius genio

geography geografía

geranium geranio

German alemán (alemana)

Germany Alemania

get (to) conseguir

get dressed (to) vestirse

get on someone's nerves (to) crispar los nervios

get up (to) levantarse

gift shop tienda de regalos

ginger jengibre

giraffe jirafa

girlfriend novia

give (to) dar

give a summons (to) denunciar

give someone a helping hand (to) echar un cable

give someone a piece of one's mind (to) cantar las cuarenta, decir cuatro cosas

give someone a taste of his own medicine (to) pagar a alguien con la misma moneda

glass vaso

glasses gafas, lentes

glorious glorioso(a)

glove guante

glove compartment guantera

glue pegamento

go (to) ir

go away (to) irse

go down (to) bajar

go out (to) salir

go over with a fine-toothed comb (to) examinar con una lupa

go to bed (early) (to) acostarse (con las gallinas)

go up (to) subir, ascender

goat cabra

godfather padrino

godmother padrina

gold oro

golf golf

good bueno(a)

good-bye adiós

goods productos

goose ganso

gorilla gorila

government gobierno

governor gobernador(a)

grade nota

graduate graduarse

graduate student estudiante graduado

grammar gramática

granddaughter nieta

grandfather abuelo

grandmother abuela

grandson nieto

grape uva

grapefruit toronja, pomelo

graphics card tarjeta gráfica

grass hierba

grate (to) rallar

gratitude gratitud

gravel grava

gravity gravedad

gray gris

gray hair canas

great regio(a), fantástico(a)

Greece Grecia

Greek griego(a)

green verde

greens verduras

greet (to) saludar

grief dolor

grind (to) moler

grocery store abacería, bodega

ground floor planta baja

group grupo

grouper mero

Guatemalan guatemalteco(a)

guess (to) adivinar

guest huésped

guilt culpa

guilty (party) culpable

guitar guitarra

gun rifle, fusil

gym gimnasio

habit hábito

hacker pirata

hail granizo

hair cabello, pelo

hair spray laca

hair stylist peluquero(a)

half gallon medio galón

half hour media hora

hall pasillo

ham jamón

hamburger hamburguesa

hammock hamaca

hand mano

handball balonmano

handful puñado

handkerchief pañuelo

handsome guapo

hang up (phone) (to)   colgar

hangar   percha

happiness   felicidad, alegría

happy   feliz, alegre, contento

hard-boiled (eggs)   duros

hard-working   trabajador

hardware store   ferretería

harmless   inofensivo(a)

harmonica   armónica

harp   arpa

hat   sombrero

hate   odio

hate (to)   odiar

have (helping verb) (to)   haber

have (to)   tener

have a free hand (to)   tener carta blanca

have a sleepless night (to)   pasar la noche en blanco

have breakfast (to)   desayunarse

have fun (to)   divertirse

have the right of way (to)   tener derecho de paso

hazel (eyes)   color de avellana

hazelnut   avellana

head   cabeza

headline   titular

health   salud

health care   asistencia médica

hear (to)   oír, entender

heart   corazón

heart attack   ataque al corazón

heat   calefacción

heat (to)   calentar

heater   calentador

heaven   cielo

heel   tacón

height   altura

help (to)   ayudar, servir

hen   gallina

her   sus, suya

here   aquí

hero   héroe

hide (to)   esconder(se), encubrir

high   alto

highlighter   marcador

highlights   reflejos

highway   autopista, carretera

hike   caminata

hill   colina

hip   cadera

hire (to)   contratar

his   sus, suyo

Hispanic   hispano(a)

history   historia

hit   jit

hit rock bottom (to)   tocar fondo

hockey   jockey

hole   roto

holiday   día de fiesta

home page   página inicial

home run   jonrón

homework   tarea

honey   miel

honeymoon   luna de miel

honor   honor

hood   capota

hoop   aro

hope   esperanza

horn   bocina

horn   cuerno

horrible   horrible

horse   caballo

horseback riding   equitación

hospital   hospital

hostile   hostil

hotel   hotel

hour   hora

house   casa

how   cómo

how much   cuántos

however   sin embargo

hug (to)   abrazar

humid   húmedo

humidity   humedad

humility   humildad

hundred   ciento (cien)

hunting   caza

hurricane   huracán

hurt (to)   doler

hurt oneself (to)   hacerse daño

husband   marido, esposo

ice   hielo

ice cream   helado

ice crusher   picahielos

ice cubes   cubitos de hielo

ice-cream parlor   heladería

icemaker   máquina de fabricar hielo

icepack   bolsa de hielo

icon   icono

identification card   tarjeta de identidad

ignition   ignición

ignorance   ignorancia

ignore (to)   ignorar

illness   enfermedad

imagination   imaginación

immediately   inmediatamente

immigration   inmigración

impatient   impaciente

imperative   imperativo

import (to)   importar

importance   importancia

important   importante

impossible   imposible

improbable   improbable

impulsive   impulsivo(a)

in back of   detrás de

in front of   delante de

in love   enamorado(a)

in the middle of   en medio de

inaction   inacción

incapable   incapaz

incertitude   incertidumbre

include (to)   incluír

incompetence incompetencia

incomprehensible incomprensible

increase (to) aumentar

incredible increíble

independence independencia

index card ficha

Indian indio(a)

indigo añil

indispensable indispensable

individual individuo

indoor pool piscina cubierta

indulgent blando(a)

inertia inercia

influence influencia

inhabitant habitante

inhibit (to) inhibir

ink tinta

inkpad almohadilla de entintar

inn hostería

innocence inocencia

insect insecto

insecure inseguro(a)

insert (to) introducir, insertar

inside dentro de

insightful perspicaz

insignificance insignificancia

insist (to) insistir

installment payment pago a plazos

installment plan facilidades de pago

institute instituto

instructor instructor(a)

insubordination indisciplina

insurance seguro

insurance policy póliza de seguros

insure (to) asegurar

intensive care unit unidad de cuidado intensivo

interest interés

interest rate el tipo de interés

interested interesado(a)

interesting interesante

intermission intermedio

interpreter intérprete

interrupt (to) interrumpir

intersection cruce

interview entrevista

intimate íntimo(a)

introspective introspectivo(a)

intuitive intuitivo(a)

invitation invitación

invite (to) invitar

Ireland Irlanda

Irish irlandés (irlandesa)

iron hierro

ironic irónico

island isla

Italian italiano(a)

Italy Italia

itinerary itinerario

ivory marfil

jack gato

jacket chaqueta

jade jade

jai alai wall frontón

jail cárcel

jam mermelada

janitor bedel

January enero

Japan Japón

Japanese japonés (japonesa)

jar pomo, frasco

jealous celoso(a)

jealousy celos

jeans vaqueros

jelly mermelada

jewel joya

jeweler joyero(a)

jewelry store joyeréa

Jewish judío(a)

job puesto

job application solicitud

jogging trotar, footing

journalist periodista

joy alegría

judge juez (jueza)

juice jugo

July julio

jump rope cuerda para brincar

June junio

jury jurado

justice justicia

kangaroo canguro

keep (to) guardar

key llave, tecla

keyboard teclado

keypad teclas

**kill two birds with one stone
(to)** matar dos pájaros de un tiro

kind amable

kindness bondad

king rey

kingdom reino

kiss (to) besar

kitchen cocina

kite cometa

kiwi kiwi

knee rodilla

kneepads rodilleras

knife cuchillo

knife sharpener afilador

know (to) saber, conocer

knowledge conocimiento

label etiqueta

laboratory laboratorio

laborer obrero(a)

lace encaje

laces cordones

lagoon laguna

lake lago

lamb carne de cordero

lamp lámpara

landing aterrizaje

landscape   paisaje

lane   carril, pista

language   lengua, idioma

laptop   computadora portátil

large   grande

last   pasado(a), último(a)

late   tarde

Latin   latino(a)

Latin   latín

Latin American   latinoamericano(a)

laugh (to)   reír(se)

laundry   lavandería

law   ley

lawn   césped

lawn chair   silla de patio

lawsuit   demanda

lawyer   abogado(a)

layered (cut)   en degradación

lazy   perezoso(a)

lead   plomo

leader   jefe, líder

leaf   hoja

learn (to)   aprender

lease   de arrendamiento contrato

leather   cuero

leather-goods store   marroquinería

leave (put down) (to)   dejar

leave (to)   partir, salir

Lebanon   Líbano

leek   puerro

left   izquierdo(a)

left (to the ___ of)   a la de izquierda

leg   pierna

legal action   denuncia

legal adviser   consejero(a) legal

legal department   departamento legal

legal settlement   acuerdo legal

legalize (to)   legalizar

legitimate   legítimo(a)

lemon   limón

lemonade   limonada

length   largo

leopard   leopardo

less   menos

lesson   lección

let one's hair down (to)   soltarse la melena

letter   carta

lettuce   lechuga

liberate (to)   liberar

librarian   bibliotecario(a)

library   biblioteca

license   permiso

license plate   placa de matrícula

lie   mentira

life   vida

lifeguard   salvavidas

lifevest   chaleco salvavidas

light   claro(a), faro, luz

light-years   años luz

lightning   relámpago

like (to) gustar

lime lima

limousine limosina

line cola

linen lino

lines líneas

lion león

lip labio

lip balm protector labial

lip gloss brillo de labios

lipstick lápiz de labios

liquid líquido

liquor store tienda de licores

listen (to) escuchar

liter litro

little poco(a)

live (to) vivir

live in style (to) vivir a todo tren

lively animado(a)

liver hígado

living room sala

loan préstamo

lobster langosta

long largo(a)

long-distance call llamada de larga distancia

look at (to) mirar

look for (to) buscar

looseleaf binder carpeta de anillos

lose (to) perder

lose one's temper (to) perder los estribos

lost and found oficina de objetos perdidos

lot mucho(a)

lotion loción

loud chillón

love amor

love (to) amar

loved amado(a)

lover amante

low bajo(a)

low-cut escotado

lower (to) bajar

luggage equipaje

lump bulto

lunch almuerzo

lung pulmón

lute laúd

luxurious lujoso(a)

luxury lujo

lyre lira

mackerel caballa

magic magia

maid service gobernanta

mail carrier cartero(a)

mailbox buzón

maintenance gastos de mantenimiento

major especialidad

major (to) especializarse

make (car) marca

make (to) hacer

make a mountain out of a molehill (to)   ahogarse en un vaso de agua

make someone's life miserable (to)   amargar la vida a alguien

make up my mind (to)   decidirse

makeup   maquillaje

makeup remover   demaquillador

mall (shopping)   centro comercial

manage (to)   administrar, manejar

management   gerencia

manager   director(a), gerente

manager   dirigente

manicure   manicura

manners   modales, ademanes

map   mapa, plano

maple   arce

maracas   maracas

marble   mármol

marbles   canicas

March   marzo

marinated   escabechado

mark (to)   marcar

market   mercado

maroon   granate

Mars   Marte

mascara   rímel

master   maestro(a)

Master's degree   master

match   partido

math   matemáticas

May   mayo

mayonnaise   mayonesa

mayor   alcalde, older

meal   comida

meanwhile   mientras tanto

measure (to)   medir

meat   carne

mechanic   mecánico(a)

medication   medicina

medium   mediano, término medio

medium-rare   poco rojo

melon   melón

melt (to)   derretir

memorize (to)   aprender de memoria

memory   memoria

memory card   carta de memoria

mend (to)   remendar

menu   menú

merchandise   mercancía

merchant   comerciante

Mercury   Mercurio

merge (to)   fusionar

message   mensaje

messy   descuidado(a)

mezzanine   entresuelo

microwave   microondas

Middle Eastern   medio-oriental

middleman   intermediario

midnight   medianoche

migraine   jaqueca

mileage   kilometraje, millaje

milk   leche

million millón

minister ministro(a)

minus menos

minute minuto

mirror espejo

missile misil

mistake falta, error

mix (to) mezclar

mixer batidora

mobile móvil

model modelo

modeling clay plasticina

modern moderno

modify (to) modificar

moisturizing hidratante

monarchy monarquía

Monday lunes

money dinero, moneda

money exchange cambio de dinero

monkey mono

monkfish rape

month mes

monthly mensual

monthly payments mensualidades

monument monumento

moon luna

more más

morning mañana

Morocco Marruecos

mortgage hipoteca

mother madre

mother-in-law suegra

motor motor

motorcycle motocicleta, moto

mountain montaña

mountain climbing alpinismo

mouse ratón

mouth boca

mouthful bocado

mouthwash enjuagador bucal

movie película

movies cine

much mucho(a)

mud barro

muggy heat bochorno

multicolored multicolor

multiply multiplicar

mumps paperas

muralist muralista

murals murales

museum museo

mushroom champiñón

music música

music store tienda de discos

musician músico(a)

Muslim musulmán

mustache bigote

mustard mostaza

mystery misterio

nail uña

nail file lima

nail polish esmalte

nail-polish remover quitaesmaltes

name nombre

napkin servilleta

narrate (to) narrar

narrow estrecho(a)

nasty antipático

nationality nacionalidad

Native American amerindio(a)

natural natural

navy azul marino

near cerca de

neat aseado

necessary necesario, preciso, menester

neck cuello

necklace collar

necktie corbata

nectarine nectarina

need (to) necesitar

nephew sobrino

Neptune Neptuno

nervous nervioso(a)

net red

Netherlands Países Bajos

network red

nevertheless sin embargo

news noticias

newspaper periódico

newspaper stand quiosco de periódicos

next próximo

Nicaraguan nicaragüense

nice bueno(a), simpático(a)

niece sobrina

night noche

nightclub club

nightstand buró

nine nueve

nineteen diecinueve

ninety noventa

ninth noveno

noise ruido

north norte

North America América del Norte

Norway Noruega

nose nariz

note (to) notar

notebook cuaderno

notice aviso, notificación

notice (to) fijarse

noun sustantivo

novel novela

November noviembre

now ahora

nowadays hoy día

number número

nurse enfermero(a)

nut nuez

nylon nylon

oak   roble

obey (to)   obedecer

oboe   oboe

observe (to)   observar, notar

obtain (to)   obtener, conseguir

obvious   obvio

occur (to)   occurir

ocean   océano

October   octubre

of course   por supuesto

offensive   ofensivo(a)

offer   oferta

office   oficina

officer   oficial

often   a menudo

oil   aceite

oil painting   pintura al óleo

okra   quimbombó

old   antiguo, viejo(a)

older   mayor

olive   oliva

omelet   tortilla

omit (to)   omitir

on   sobre

on the corner of   en la esquina de

on the peak of   en la cima de

on time   a tiempo

one   uno(a)

one-way   único de sentido

onion   cebolla

online services   servicios en línea

onyx   ónice

opal   ópalo

open   abierto(a)

open (to)   abrir

opera   ópera

operating room   sala de opera-ciones

operating system   sistema opera-tivo

operating table   mesa de opera-ciones

operator   operador(a)

opposite   enfrente de

opposite direction   dirección contraria (opuesta)

optical store   óptica

optician   óptico(a)

optimistic   optimista

opulence   opulencia

orange   anaranjado, naranja

orbit   órbita

orchestra   orquesta

orchestra section   patio

order (to)   mandar, ordenar

organ   órgano

organize (to)   organizar

originality   originalidad

ostentatious   ostentoso(a)

out of order   fuera de servicio

out of this world   de película

outer space   espacio exterior

outfielder   jardinero

outside   afuera, fuera de

outskirts   afueras

outstanding   notable

oven   horno

overcast   cubierto

overcoat   abrigo

overcooked   sobrecocido dulce

overdrawn (check)   sin fondos

overtime   horas extraordinarias (suplementarias) either

overtime pay   sobresueldo

owner   dueño(a), propietario

oyster   ostra

pacifier   chupete

package   paquete

paella   paella

page   página

pain   dolor, pena

paint   pintura

paint (to)   pintar

painter   pintor(a)

painting   cuadro

pajamas   pijamas

Panamanian   panameño(a)

panic   pánico

panther   pantera

pants   pantalón

pantyhose   pantimedias

paper   papel

paperclip   sujetapapel

paprika   pimentón

parade   desfile

Paraguayan   paraguayo(a)

parallel   paralelo

park   parque

park (to)   estacionar, aparcar

parking lot   estacionamiento

parsley   perejil

parsnip   pastinaca

partner   socio

part-time   tiempo parcial

party   partido

passenger   pasajero(a)

passionate   apasionado(a)

passport   pasaporte

pastel   pastel

pastry shop   pastelería

patience   paciencia

patio   patio

pay (to)   pagar

pay attention (to)   prestar atención

pay cash (to)   pagar en efectivo, pagar al contado

payment   pago

peace   paz

peach   melocotón

peanut   cacahuete, maní

pear   pera

pear tree   peral

pearl   perla

peas   guisantes

pedestrian   peatón (peatona)

pedicure   pedicura

peel (to) pelar

pen pluma

pen (ball-point) bolígrafo

pen (fountain) pluma

pencil lápiz

pencil case estuche

pencil sharpener sacapuntas

peninsula península

pension pensión

pepper (black) pimienta

pepper (red) pimiento, ají

pepper shaker pimentero

per por

percent porcentaje

percentage porcentaje

perfect perfecto

performance función

perfume perfume

perfume shop perfumería

perhaps tal vez

perimeter perímetro

peripherals periféricos

permanent permanente

permit (to) permitir

persevere (to) perseverar

persist (to) persistir

person persona

personality personalidad

personnel personal

perspective perspectiva

persuade (to) persuadir

peso weight

pessimistic pesimista

pharmacist farmacéutico(a)

phone bill cuenta del teléfono

phone card tarjeta telefónica

photographer fotógrafo

phrase frase

physics física

piano piano

piccolo flautín

pick up (phone) (to) descolgar

pick up (to) recoger

pickles encurtidos

picnic picnic

picture cuadro, pintura, retrato

pie pastel

piece trozo, pedazo

pier muelle

pig cerdo

pillow almohada

pilot piloto

pin broche

pine pino

pineapple piña

pink rosado(a)

pint pinta

pit (of orchestra) foso

pity lástima

place setting cubiertos

plain (omelet) a la francesa

plaintiff demandante

plan (to) planear, planificar

planet planeta

planetary nebula nebulosa planetaria

plant planta

plantain plátano

plate plato

play obra teatral

play (instrument) (to) tocar

play (sport) (to) jugar

player jugador

playpen corral de juego

pleasant agradable

pleasure gusto, placer

plot trama

plum ciruela

plumber plomero(a)

plus más

Pluto Plutón

pneumonia pulmonía

poached escalfado

pocket bolsillo

pocketbook cartera

poet poeta (poetisa)

Poland Polonia

pole palo

police policía

police officer policía

police station comisaría

police story historia policíaca

political prisoner preso político

politics política

pollution contaminación

polyester poliéster

pomegranate granada

pond charca

pool (swimming) piscina

popcorn palomitas de maíz

population población

pork cerdo

port puerto

porter portero

Portuguese portugués (portuguesa)

pose posar

possess poseer

possible posible

post office correo

Post-its notas adhesivas

post-office box apartado postal, casilla postal

post-office worker cartero

postage franqueo

postal zone zona postal, código postal

postcard tarjeta postal

postmark matasellos

pot olla

potato papa

pothole bache

poultry aves

pound libra

pour (to) verter

poverty pobreza

powder polvo

power poder

power surge parasito violento

practical práctico

practice (to) practicar

precious precioso(a)

prefer (to) preferir

preferable preferible

prepare (to) preparar

prescription receta

present presente

president presidente (presidenta)

press prensa

press (clothing) (to) planchar

pretty bonito(a)

price precio

pride orgullo

priest cura

prince príncipe

princess princesa

principal director

print (to) imprimir

prison prisión

probable probable

problem problema

producer productor

profession profesión

profit ganancias

program programa

programmer programador(a)

prohibit (to) prohibir

prohibited prohibido

pronounce (to) pronunciar

property propiedad

protect oneself (to) protejerse

Protestant protestante

proud orgulloso(a)

prove (to) probar

prudent prudente

prune ciruela pasa

psychologist psicólogo(a)

puck disco

pudding natilla, pudín

Puerto Rican puertorriqueño(a)

pullover suéter

pulse pulso

punish (to) castigar

punishment castigo, punición

pupil alumno (alumna)

puppets títeres

purifier (water) depuradora

purple morado, púrpura

put (on) (to) poner

put on (clothing) (to) ponerse

put on makeup (to) maquillarse

**put one's cards on the table
(to)** poner las cartas sobre la mesa

**put something on burner
(to)** poner al fuego

puzzle rompecabezas

qualification aptitud, competencia

quart cuartillo, cuarto

quarter cuarto

quarter of an hour cuarto de hora

queen reina

question pregunta

quite bastante

quiz prueba

quotient cociente

rabbi rabí, rabino(a)

rabbit conejo

racing carreras

racism racismo

racket raqueta

radiator radiador

radio radio

radish rábano

radius radio

rage cólera

railroad ferrocarril

rain lluvia

rain (to) llover

rain cats and dogs (to) llover a cántaros

raise (to) levantar, elevar

raisin pasa

rapidity rapidez

rare raro(a)

rare (meat) poco asado

rash erupción

raspberry frambuesa, mora

rate tarifa

rather bastante

rattle sonajero

razor rasuradora

razor blade hoja de afeitar

read between the lines (to) leer entre líneas

reading lectura

real estate bienes raíces

real-estate agency inmobiliaria agencia

realism realismo

reality realidad

rearview mirror retrovisor

receipt recibo

receive (to) recibir

receiver auricular

reception recepción

recite (to) recitar

recover recuperar

recovery room sala de recuperación, restablecimiento

rectify (to) rectificar

red rojo

redhead pelirrojo(a)

reduce (to) reducir por cocción

references referencias

refined fino(a), culto(a)

reflect (to) reflejar

refrigerator refrigerador

refuge asilo, refugio

regret (to) pesar

regrettable lamentable

regular mail correo ordinario

relax (to) relajarse

relaxed relajado(a)

religion religión

religiousness religioso

remain (to) quedarse

remember (to) acordarse, recordar

remorse remordimiento

remove (to) quitar(se)

remove something (to) retirar

renounce (to) renunciar

renown renombre

rent alquilar

repair (to) reparar

repeat (to) repetir

repel (to) rechazar

represent (to) representar

republic república

researcher investigador(a)

reservation reserva

reserve (to) reservar

resident residente

resist (to) resistir

respect respeto

respect (to) venerar, respetar

respectful respetuoso(a)

respond (to) responder

responsible responsable

rest (to) descansar

restaurant restaurante

restless inquieto(a)

result resultado

resumé historial

return (to) regresar, volver

reveal (to) revelar

review repaso, crítica

reviewer crítico(a)

revolt rebelión

revolve (to) girar

reward recompensa

reward (to) premiar

rice arroz

richness riqueza

ride (a bicycle) (to) montar

ridiculous ridículo(a)

rifle fusil

right derecho(a)

right (to the ___ of) a la derecha de

right now ahora mismo

rights derechos

ring (jeweled) sortija

ring (plain) anillo

rink pista

rite rito

river río

road camino

road sign rótulo

roast (to) asar

roast beef rosbíf

robe bata

rock piedra

rocket cohete

rod caña

role papel

roller rolo

rolls panecillos

romantic romántico(a)

roof techo

room cuarto, habitación, sala

rooster gallo

root raíz

rose rosa, rosado(a)

rosemary romero

round off (to) redondear

route ruta

row fila

rowing remo

rubber caucho

rubber band goma

ruby rubí

rug alfombra

rule regla

ruler regla

run carrera

run (to) correr

Russian ruso(a)

sacrifice sacrificio

sad triste

sadness tristeza

safe (deposit box) caja fuerte

safety seguridad

safety pin seguro

saffron azafrán

sailing navegación

salad ensalada

salary sueldo

sale ganga

salesperson dependiente

salmon salmón

salt sal

salt shaker salero

sample muestra

sample (to) probar

sand arena

sandals sandalias

sandwich sándwich

sapphire zafiro

sardine sardina

satellite satélite

satin raso

Saturday sábado

Saturn Saturno

sauce salsa

saucepan cacerola

saucer platillo

sauerkraut chucrut

sausage salchicha

sauté (to) saltear

save (to) ahorrar

saxophone saxofón

say (to) decir

say good-bye despedirse

say something without really meaning it (to) decir algo con la boca chica

scale báscula

scallop vieira

scan (to) barrer

scandalous escandaloso(a)

scar cicatriz

scarf pañuelo, bufanda

scene escena

schedule horario

school escuela

school supplies útiles

science ciencia

science fiction ciencia ficción

scientist científico(a)

scissors tijeras

score anotación

scoreboard marcador

Scotland Escocia

Scottish escocés (escocesa)

scrambled (eggs) revueltos

screen pantalla

scuba diving buceo

sculptor escultor(a)

sculpture escultura

sea mar

seafood mariscos

seagull gaviota

search engine buscador

season estación

season (to) sazonar

season ticket entrada de abono

seat asiento

seat (baby) sillita

seat (to) sentar

seat belt cinturón de seguridad

second segundo

secretary secretario(a)

security seguridad

security check control de seguridad

security guard guardia de seguridad

see (to) ver

seed semilla

seldom rara vez

selfish egoísta

sell (to) vender

seller vendedor(a)

senate senado

send (to) enviar, mandar

send back (to) devolver

sender remitente

sensational sensacional

sensitive sensible

sentence oración

September septiembre

serious serio(a)

server mozo(a), mesero(a), servidor(a)

service servicio

sesame ajonjolí

set marcado(a), decorado(a)

set (to) reposar

settle (to) saldar, liquidar

seven siete

seventeen diecisiete

seventh séptimo

seventy setenta

sewing machine máquina de coser

shade tono

shades, blinds persianas

shadow sombra

shame vergüenza

shampoo champú

share (to) compartir

shark tiburón

shave (to) afeitar(se)

shaving cream crema de afeitar

sheep oveja

sheet of stamps hoja de sellos

shell concha

shine (to) brillar, lucir

shipment envío

shirt camisa

shiver (to) temblar

shoe zapato

shoestore zapatería

shoemaker's zapatería

shore orilla

short corto(a)

shortly dentro de poco

shoulder hombro

shout (to) gritar

show exposición

show (movie) (to) pasar

show (to) mostrar, enseñar

show one's true colors (to) enseñar el cobre

shower ducha

shower llovizna

shrimp camarones, gambas

shy tímido(a)

sick enfermo(a)

side lado

side street bocacalle

sideburns patillas

sign (to) firmar

signal (to) señalizar, avisar

silence silencio

silence (to) silenciar, callar

silk seda

silly tonto(a)

silver plata

simple simple

simplicity sencillez

simplify simplificar

since desde

sincere sincero(a)

sing (to) cantar

sink (bathroom) lavabo; (kitchen) fregadero

sister hermana

sister-in-law cuñada

sit (to) sentarse

six seis

sixteen dieciséis

sixth sexto

sixty sesenta

size (clothing) talla

size (shoes) número

skateboard monopatín

skates patines

skating patinaje

skiing esquí

skin piel

skirt falda

sky cielo

sled trineo

sleep (to) dormir

sleepy soñoliento(a)

slice trozo

slice (bread) (to) rebanar

slip (full) combinación

slip (half) faldellín

slip (to) resbalar(se)

slippers (bedroom) pantuflas

slot ranura

slow lento(a)

slowly despacio

slowness lentitud

small pequeño(a)

smell (to) oler

smoke detector detector de humo

snack merienda

snails caracoles

snake serpiente

sneakers tenis

sneeze estornudar

snow nieve

snow (to) nevar

so tan

soak (to) remojar

soap jabón

soap opera telenovela

soccer fútbol

socks calcetines

soda gaseosa

sofa sofá

soft drinks refrescos

soft-boiled (eggs) pasados por agua

soil tierra

solar system sistema solar

sole (fish) lenguado

sole (shoe) suela

solid sólido

solution solución

solve (to) resolver

some unos

someone alguien

something algo

sometimes a veces

son hijo

song canción

son-in-law yerno

soon pronto

soup sopa

soup dish sopera

soup spoon cuchara

south sur

South America Sudamérica

souvenir shop tienda de recuerdos

space espacio

space capsule cápsula espacial

spaceship nave espacial

Spain España

Spanish español(a)

spare tire goma de repuesto (recambio)

speak (to) hablar

speaker phone teléfono altavoz

special especial

special-delivery letter carta urgente

specialist especialista

speed velocidad

spell checker el verificador de ortografía

spelling ortografía

spice especia

spicy picante

spinach espinaca

sponge esponja

sponge cake bizcocho

sport deporte

sporting-goods stores tienda de equipo deportivo

sporty deportivo(a)

sprain torcedura

spreadsheet hoja de cálculo electrónica

spring primavera

square cuadrado, plaza

squash calabaza

squirrel ardilla

stadium estadio

staff funcionarios

stage escenario, escena

stain mancha

staircase escalera

stairs escalera(s)

stamp sello

stand up (to) levantarse

stapler grapadora

star estrella

starch (to) almidonar

start (car) (to) arrancar

start from scratch (to) empezar de cero

stationery objetos de escritorio

stature (height) estatura

steak bistec

steal (to) robar

steamed al vapor

steel acero

steering wheel volante

stem tallo

stepbrother hermanastro

stepdaughter hijastra

stepfather padrastro

stepmother madrastra

stepsister hermanastra

stepson hijastro

stereo estéreo

stew estofado, guisado

stewardess azafata

still todavía

stir (to) revolver

stitches puntos, suturas

stockings medias

stomach estómago

stone piedra

stop (to) parar(se)

stop over escala

store tienda

storm tormenta, tempestad

stormy tormentoso(a)

story (floor) piso

storybook libro de cuentos

stout pesado(a)

stove estufa

straight liso(a), recto(a), derecho(a)

straighten (to) alisar

strain (to) colar

strange extraño

straw paja

strawberry fresa

stream arroyo

street calle

stress estrés

stretcher camilla

strict rígido(a)

strike huelga

string cordón

stroke ataque de apoplejía

stroller carrito de bebé

strong fuerte

structure estructura

student alumno(a), estudiante

student's desk pupitre

study estudio

study (to) estudiar

stuffed animal animal de peluche

style peinado, estilo

subject materia

subtitles subtítulos

subtract (to) restar

subway metro

suddenly de repente

sue (to) demandar

suede gamuza

suffer (to) sufrir

sugar azúcar

suit traje

suitcase maleta

sum suma

summary resumen

summer verano

sun sol

sun hat sombrero de ala ancha

sunbathing baño de sol

sunblock filtro solar

sunburn quemadura de sol

Sunday domingo

sunglasses gafas de sol

sunny soleado

sunstroke insolación

suntan bronceado

suntan lotion loción bronceadora

super genial

superb espléndido(a)

superintendent superintendente

supermarket supermercado

supervisor supervisor(a)

supply and demand oferta y demanda

sure cierto(a), seguro(a)

surfboard tabla de surf

surfer surfista

surfing surfing

surgeon cirujano(a)

surprise sorpresa

surprised sorprendido(a)

surprising sorprendente

surrealist surrealista

suspicious sospechoso(a), suspicaz

swan cisne

sweat (to) sudar, transpirar

sweater suéter

Sweden Suecia

Swedish sueco(a)

sweet dulce

sweet potato batata, camote

sweetheart corazoncito(a)

swelling inflamación

swim (to) nadar

swimming natación

swimming pool piscina

Swiss suizo(a)

Switzerland Suiza

sword espada

synagogue sinagoga

syrup jarabe

table mesa

tablecloth mantel

tablespoon cucharada

taciturn taciturno(a)

taffeta tafetán

tag (luggage) etiqueta

tailor sastre (costurera)

take (to) coger, tomar

take a shower (to) ducharse

take notes (to) tomar apuntes

take off (remove) (to) quitarse

take the bull by the horns (to) coger el toro por los cuernos

takeoff despegue

talent genio

talkative hablador(a)

tambourine pandereta

tame doméstico(a)

tangerine   mandarina

tapas   tapas

tape backup   cinta de seguridad

tart   tarta

tasty   sabroso

tax   carga, impuesto

taxi   taxi

tea   té

teacher (elementary)   maestro(a)

teacher (secondary)   profesor(a)

team   equipo

tear   desgarrón

teaspoon   cucharita, cucharadita

technician   técnico(a)

technology   tecnología

teddy bear   osito de peluche

telephone   teléfono

telephone (to)   telefonear

telephone bill   cuenta del teléfono

telephone book   guía telefónica

telephone booth   cabina telefónica

telephone company   compañía telefónica

telephone line   línea de teléfono

telephone number   número de teléfono

television announcer   locutor(a) de televisión

television set   televisor

tell (to)   decir, contar

teller   cajero(a)

temperature   temperatura

temple   templo

ten   diez

tenant   inquilino

tennis   tenis

tenth   décimo

terminal   terminal

terrace   terraza

terrible   terrible

terrific   fenomenal

terror   terror

terrorism   terrorismo

test   examen

testimony   testimonio

textbook   libro de texto

theater   teatro

theme   tema

therapist   terapista

there   allá

there is (are)   hay

thermometer   termómetro

thesaurus   diccionario de sinónimos

they   ellos, ellas

thicken (to)   espesar

thin   delgado(a), flaco(a)

think (to)   pensar

third   tercero

thirteen   trece

thirty   treinta

thoroughly   a fondo

thousand   mil

three tres

throat garganta

throw (to) lanzar, tirar

throw in the towel (to) tirar la toalla

thumbtacks tachuelas

thunder trueno

thunder (to) tronar

Thursday jueves

ticket boleto, billete

ticket window ventanilla

tiger tigre

tight (clothing) apretado(a)

tight (shoes) estrechos

time hora, tiempo

timer temporizador

times por

time-sharing copropiedad

tip propina

tire goma, llanta

tired cansado(a)

tissues pañuelos de papel

toast (to) brindar

toaster tostadora

tobacco store tabaquería

together juntos

toilet paper papel higiénico

tolerate (to) tolerar, soportar

toll peaje

tollbooth cabina de peaje

tomato tomate

tongue lengua

too (much) demasiado

tooth diente

toothpaste pasta dentífrica

top trompo

top (of tree) copa

topaz topacio

total monto

touch (to) tocar

touch-tone phone teléfono de botones

tourism turismo

toward hacia

town hall ayuntamiento

toy juguete

toy chest baúl de juguetes

toystore juguetería

track carrera

traffic tránsito

traffic jam embotellamiento

traffic light semáforo

traffic signal señal

tragedy tragedia

tragic trágico(a)

train tren

train station estación

tranquilo calm

transfer transferencia, correspondencia

transfer (to) transferir

translator traductor(a)

transmission transmisión

transmit (to) transmitir

transport (to) transportar

trapped atrapado(a)

trash compactor compactador de basuras

travel (to) viajar

traveler viajero(a)

tray table bandeja

treasure tesoro

treaty tratado

tree árbol

trial juicio

triangle triángulo

tricycle triciclo

trim (to) recortar

trip viaje

triumph (to) triunfar

trombone trombón

trout trucha

truck camión

true verdad

trumpet trompeta

trunk baúl

trunk (tree) tronco

trust confianza

truth verdad

T-shirt camiseta

Tuesday martes

tulip tulipán

tuna atún

Tunisia Túnez

turkey pavo

Turkey Turquía

turn doblar

turn around dar la vuelta

turn off (to) apagar

turn on (to) encender, poner en marcha

turnip nabo

turquoise turquesa

turtle tortuga

tuxedo esmoquin

tweezers pinzas

twelve doce

twenty veinte

twenty-one veintiuno

twig ramita

twinkle (to) centellear

two dos

two hundred doscientos

type especie

ugly feo(a)

ukulele ukelele

umbrella paraguas

umpire árbitro

unbearable insoportable

unbelievable increíble

uncle tío

uncover (to) destapar

under bajo

understand (to) comprender

unfair injusto

unforgettable inolvidable

ungrateful ingrato(a)

unhappiness desdicha

unhappy triste

union sindicato, unión

unit unidad

United States Estados Unidos

universe universo

university universidad

until hasta

upon sobre

upset molesto(a)

Uranus Urano

urgent urgente

use, purpose uso, empleo

use (to) usar, utilizar, emplear

useful útil

user usuario(a)

usher guía

usher (theater) acomodador(a)

vacation vacaciones

vaccination vacuna

vacuum cleaner aspiradora

valet parking atendencia del garaje

value valor

van camioneta

vanity vanidad

VCR video(casetera)

veal ternera

vegetable verdura, legumbre

vehicle vehículo

veil velo

velvet terciopelo

Venezuelan venezolano(a)

venison venado

Venus Venus

verb verbo

verdict veredicto

very muy

very early morning madrugada

very rare casi crudo

vest chaleco

vice vicio

video game juego de computadora

video shop videoclub

view vista

vinegar vinagre

viola viola

violence violencia

violent violento(a)

violet violeta

violin violén

vitamins vitaminas

vocabulary vocabulario

voicemail buzón de voz

void inválido(a)

volleyball voleibol

vote voto

vote (to) votar

vow prometer

waffle maker waflera

wagon vagón

wait (to) esperar

waiter mozo, camarero

wake up (to) despertarse

walk paseo

walk (to) caminar, marchar

walk down the aisle (to) caminar al altar

wall pared

wallet cartera

walnut nuez

walnut tree nogal

want (to) querer

war guerra

wardrobe armario, guardarropa

warn (to) advertir, prevenir

wash (to) lavar(se)

washing machine lavadora

waste (to) gastar

wastepaper basket cesto de papeles

watch reloj

watch (to) mirar

watch band pulso

water agua

water (to) regar

water wings flotadores para los brazos

watercolor pintura de acuarela

waterfall cáscada

watermelon sandía

waterskiing esquí acuático

wave ola, onda

wavy ondulado(a)

wax crayon pintura de cera

waxing depilación

weak débil

wealth riqueza

weapons armas

weather pronóstico

weave (to) tejer

wedding boda

wedding cake torta (pastel) de boda

wedding day día de bodas

wedding dress traje de novia

wedding ring anillo de matrimonio, alianza

Wednesday miércoles

weed out (to) arrancar

weigh (to) pesar

weight peso

weight lifting levantamiento de pesas

weight training entrenamiento con pesas

well-done bien cocido

well-mannered educado(a)

west oeste

wet húmedo(a)

wetsuit escafandra

whale ballena

wheel rueda

wheelchair silla de ruedas

where dónde

while (a) rato (un)

white blanco(a)

white-haired canoso(a)

wide ancho(a)

wife esposa

wild salvaje

willingly de buena gana

win (to) ganar

wind viento

window ventana, ventanilla, escaparate

windshield wiper limpiaparabrisas

windstorm vendaval

windsurfing windsurfing

wine vino

wine glass copa

winter invierno

wipe (baby) toallita

wisdom sabiduría

wise sagaz

with con

with herbs con hierbas

withdraw (to) sacar, retirar

without sin

without salt sin sal

without sugar sin azúcar

witness testigo(a)

wolf lobo

wonder asombro

wonderful maravilloso(a)

wood madera

woods bosque

wool lana

word palabra

word processor procesador de textos

work obra, trabajo

work (to) trabajar, laborar, funcionar

work ethic ética de trabajo

work like a dog (to) trabajar como un burro

work shift turno

workday jornada

worker trabajador(a), empleado(a)

workplace lugar de trabajo

workstation estación de trabajo

workweek semana laboral

world mundo

worried preocupado(a), inquieto(a)

worry preocupación

worry (to) preocupar(se), inquietar(se)

worse peor

wrap (to) envolver

wrapping paper   papel de
envolver

wrestling   lucha libre

wrist   muñeca

write (to)   escribir

writer   escritor(a)

writing pad   bloc de papel

wrong (number)   equivocado

x-ray   radiografía

xylophone   xilófono

yam   camote

yellow   amarillo

yesterday   ayer

yield (produce) (to)   producir

yield (to)   ceder el paso

yogurt   yogur

young   joven

younger   menor

zebra   cebra

zero   cero

zither   cítara

zoo   parque zoológico

zucchini   calabacín